The World of Puppets

*Mechanical puppet by the Tyrolese Christian
Tschuggmall, built about 1828. Similar figures were shown
in the nineteenth century during exhibitions such as the
Teatro d'Arte Meccanico ("Mechanical Art Theater").
Designed as a moving figure in a shooting gallery, this
example is still in working order today (PM).*

The World of PUPPETS

RENÉ SIMMEN
Photographs by LEONARDO BEZZOLA

THOMAS Y. CROWELL COMPANY
Established 1834   New York

Copyright © 1972 by Silva, Zurich.
Translation copyright © 1975 by
Thomas Y. Crowell Company, Inc.

Designed by Abigail Moseley

PRINTED IN BELGIUM
by OFFSET VAN DEN BOSSCHE

Manufactured in the United States of America

Library of Congress Cataloging in Publication Data

Simmen, René.

    The world of puppets.
    Translation of Die Welt im Puppenspiel.
    Bibliography: p.
    1. Puppets and puppet-plays.   I. Title.
PN1972.S4813   791.5′3′09   75–20365

ISBN 0–690–01005–2

1 2 3 4 5 6 7 8 9 10

ACKNOWLEDGEMENTS

I would like to thank The Basil Ethnological Museum (VB); The Swiss Theatrical Collection of Bern (ST); The Munich Puppet Theater Collection (PM); The International Marionette Museum of Lyons (ML); The Zurich Museum of Arts and Trades (KJ); the Louvre (L), and private owners of theatrical puppets (PP) for permitting us to photograph their collections. A special thanks to Fred Mayer of Zurich, for photos on pages 74 and 75 and to Jacques Brunet of Berlin, for the photos on pages 110 and 113. My special appreciation to the Central Library of Zurich and to the library of the Zurich School of Arts and Trades; also to Mark Pinkus and Albert Knobel for their scientific work in this field, which they kindly lent to me, and for their iconographic material. I also want to thank Dr. Dieter Bachmann for his critical editing of this book, and all the others who have helped and advised me.

René Simmen

CONTENTS

Introduction

Pinocchio, favorite of children, was a puppet that came to life. He could walk and talk by himself. He could live and act without another's hand to guide him, a vivid image of an art so brilliant it seems to be life itself. But Pinocchio was magical. And even he found life only through the love of the man who created him.

What would a puppet show be without the creator of the puppets, and the puppeteer who maneuvers them, making them talk, sing and dance? Without the puppeteer, the puppet would end up forgotten in some dark corner as merely a toy for children or a collector's item. The puppets come to life only in the hands of the puppeteer. From him they receive body and soul, and thanks to his talent they become independent beings, the center of an artistic presentation that makes us ignore the puppeteer himself.

We do not know who was the first puppeteer. An early hypothesis is that someone observing a child at play with his doll might have had the idea of transforming that child's toy into something more dramatic.

However, dolls have existed for thousands of years. Perhaps more important than dolls were the various display figurines that our ancestors made for the dead (representing their ancestors and gods, or fetishes of revenge and fertility). Perhaps the puppet show was born not as a function of recreation but as a cult observance. Ancient priests and witches knew the effect that moving figurines had over their fol-

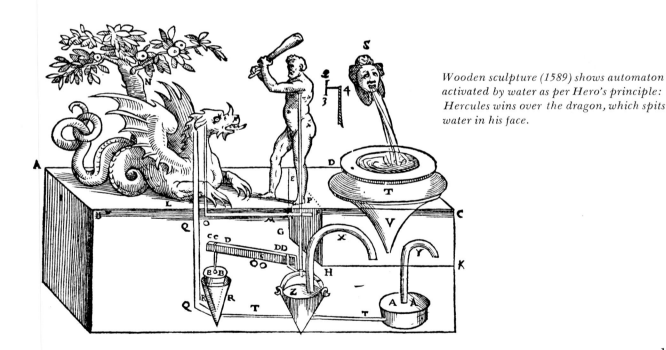

Wooden sculpture (1589) shows automaton activated by water as per Hero's principle: Hercules wins over the dragon, which spits water in his face.

1

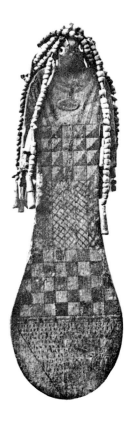

1

2

3

lowers. Even today primitive people in Africa and Australia use moving figurines in religious observances. And in some Scandinavian legends we learn of divine images believed to have life.

The first figurines were moved by hand. Later on the movements were achieved mechanically. These mechanisms (early forms of the ingenious automatons built in the eighteenth and nineteenth centuries by Vaucanson, the Jaquet-Droz brothers, Kintzing, Roentgen, Robert-Houdin, and Alois Meggenberger) were activated by the weight of water, sand, or mercury. The automatons built by Hero of Alexandria (who lived sometime between the second century B.C. and the third century A.D.) were activated by water pressure, warm air, and steam. Hero also created moving figures that, by means of strings and weights,

could represent an homage to Bacchus. From Herodotus (c. 484–425 B.C.) we learn that during the Osiris festivals the women priests carried around statues which had moving arms activated by strings. Dio Cassius (c. A.D. 155–230) tells of Egyptian statues that poured blood. The god Manducus, who was believed to eat children, was carried in Roman processions represented by a statue which had a mouth that could be opened and closed. There is ample evidence that such automated figurines did indeed exist in the ancient temples. We have the word of Aristotle, Homer, and Petronius, as well as what we have learned from Indian, Oriental, and Byzantine sources.[1] Even the Christian Church of Constantinople and the Church of the Middle Ages used these illusory methods to help their priests. As early

2

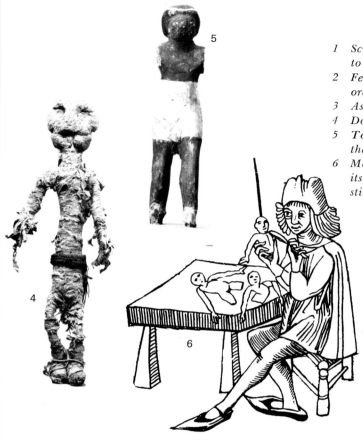

as the seventh century, figurines representing Christ, the Virgin Mary, and saints which could be moved by strings must have been common. The Crucifix of Boxley, on which the figure of Christ could move its mouth and eyes—believed the work of the devil— was destroyed in 1538. In Aix-la-Chapelle there is a wooden donkey carrying a Christ who had a moving arm. The Cluny Museum in Paris has a fifteenth-century representation of the Cross with Christ having moving eyes. Only the Reformation was able to get rid of such puppets, which had been part of the major religious observances in the English churches. In France they were used until the seventeenth century.

By that time there were already people who went around giving shows which were completely mech-anized. In 1587 the Council of Nuremberg gave Daniel Bertel from Lübeck a three-day permit "to show his tricks and his mechanisms representing a galley's navigation and battles of Turks and Christians, as well as gay Latin and German dances. All this for the reasonable price of one pfennig." In 1611 "two foreign comedians, who had brought with them several figures that moved on their own," were given a permit to stay in the city for three days. In 1702, also in Nuremberg, Gottfried Hautsch created a mechanical carousel for the court. With the help of hundreds of movements, he represented the labor of many manual workers in a display he called "Small World."[2] This is one of the many automatic presentations, known as "Theatrum Mundi," that for a long time served as the great finale in traveling

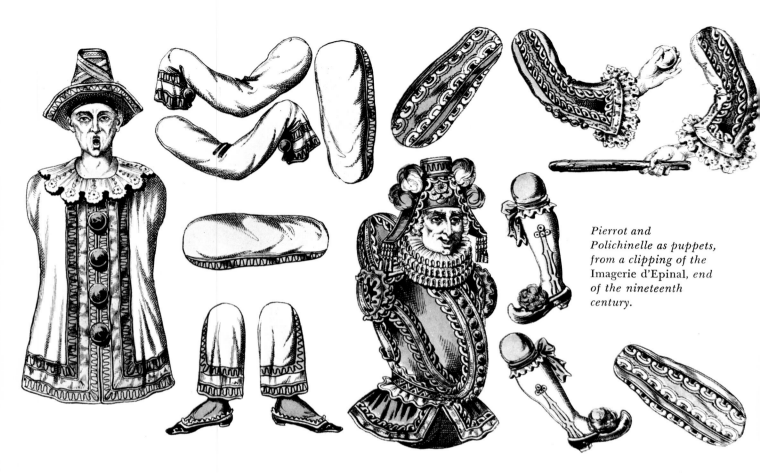

Pierrot and Polichinelle as puppets, from a clipping of the Imagerie d'Epinal, end of the nineteenth century.

marionette shows. Other rare presentations included "The Creation of the World" and "Noah and the Flood." Later in the nineteenth century battles, slaves at work, and tempests at sea were allowed to be represented.

Even today, during Christmastime, one can admire on the Piazza del Duomo in Milan, and in front of many other churches throughout Italy, the mechanical crèche. This is, of course, partly created with plastic figurines which move on tracks and are bought in a department store.

Other representations of the nativity story are Herod's soldiers in search of Jesus and scenes reproduced from old Bethlehem: women working in the mill, peasants plowing the land, and one of the wise kings, Balthazar, wearing a rich turban. This tradi-

tion was first introduced by Pope Liberius in 354. Soon afterward these nativity scenes spread all over Europe. Many churches began to compete. Their rich crèches were sometimes imported from Naples and Sicily and were incomparable for their magnificence and rich ornaments. The heads were made of terra cotta, with glass eyes; the hands and feet were made of wood, painted, like the head, in the most beautiful colors. The costumes were made from expensive materials, and the jewels were often silver or even gold. The creator of these nativity scenes had no limit in choosing characters: soldiers, princes, peasants, peddlers, shopkeepers, shepherds, children at play, beggars, and merchants. Pious people and commoners were represented in a fascinating setting with common and exotic animals. Nativity scenes

In front: popular types. In the rear: paladins of the Ciancès Theater of Liège. They are hung on a steel bar; arms and legs are activated by twisting the puppet. During the sixteenth and seventeenth centuries, similar puppets could be found everywhere in the Spanish domain from Flanders, Brussels, and Liège to Naples and Sicily. The stories of the Ciancès theater, like those of the Sicilian Opera dei Pupi, are mostly legends based on Charlemagne and his paladins. Only in Liège do they have a popular character, typified by the cheerful and quarrelsome Ciancès. The puppets differ in size according to their social standing: A worker is twenty-four inches tall, a paladin or king a little taller; Charlemagne measures more than forty-six inches (PM).

made north of the Alps could not compete with this magnificence. However, they had the ingenuity of the artists in their favor. Peasants and alpine hunters carved their own figurines and for years, during the long winter evenings, continued to make new ones, since a nativity is never really finished. There are, in fact, nativities which have taken more than a century for their completion.

The "New Diorama of Bethlehem," built around 1890 in Einsiedeln, is considered one of the most realistic nativities. It realistically reproduces the geographical setting of the Holy Land at the time of Christ's birth. The figures are carved from wood and are richly dressed. As in the old Italian crèches, the figurines can be adjusted to be shown in any desired position.

Yet this is not a puppet show. Nor are the gigantic statues carried by many men during some processions in Viareggio or the Fiesta of San Fermin in Pamplona considered puppets. Neither the lead soldiers, nor the pretty theater of cut paper, made to imitate old operas, are a puppet show. They could well be transformed into one if strings were attached to the figures to make them move. A puppet show is not one where the puppets can have their hands moved by pulling from the bottom. It is not even the cast-iron little boy who moves his head with gratitude every time a coin is put into the collection at some missionary's poor box. It is not the animated midgets and teddy bears exposed in some display window, or the saints or clowns attached to some mechanical clock. A puppet show can be defined as any dramatic form in which direct or indirect manual manipulation is used to move flat, low-relief, or high-relief figures. The main categories are:

The real puppets: consisting of a head, clothes, and arms, which are slipped over one of the puppeteer's hands. Usually the head is moved by the index or middle finger, the arms by the thumb and the little finger. The figure suddenly acquires life when someone's hand moves it. The talking and the movements are done simultaneously, just as they are with the mimic puppet, that is, with the puppeteer's hand covered by a cloth or a glove. The movements of the fingers brought together change the expressions of the face.

Marionettes: flexible puppets moved by just one rod fixed on the head, letting the figure hang loose; the arms and legs are moved by the force of gravity or by small ropes and metallic wires. The movements of rod puppets are guided from beneath through the use of rods. In special types, the movements can be attained by semi-mechanical means.

Shadow figures: flat, opaque figures which are mostly moved from beneath by small rods behind a screen. They are similar to the transparent, colored shadow figures from Asia and Turkey.

Puppet shows are also the gracious "marionettes on a small board" (*marionnettes aux genoux* or *marionnettes à la planchette*). Two puppets are placed, one in front of the other, on a small board, with a rope passing through them, and one end tied to the leg of the operator. From the movements of the operator's leg the puppets dance. A primitive form, these marionettes were still being used at the beginning of the nineteenth century by the Savoyard shepherds. This type of puppet can still be bought as a toy from some street vendors in Sicily.

Richard Pischel is inclined to think that puppet shows originated in India and gypsies brought them to the West.[3] This evolution in the West, however, can only be verified for the shadow show. Many believe that the origin of the shadow show is China and not India. Puppet and marionette shows are believed by some to have originated in Greece. In fact, they not only appeared in Greek theaters but also at the marketplace and in the streets. The pleasure of the puppet show was preserved by the Romans, who passed it along to us.[4]

In addition to comedies, the puppeteers used to perform works derived from history, from the world of legend, and also religious shows. Since the beginning of the evolution of the puppet show, the hand puppets appealed to the simple taste of the masses, while the marionette and shadow shows could portray more intellectual works. The possibil-

6

Marionette from Rajasthan, north India, nineteenth century. This kind still exists today, in addition to many others. India is a country that makes extensive use of true puppets, marionettes, and shadow shows. The word sūtradthāra *("the string holder") indicates the puppeteer, whose presence is documented since the tenth century. However, there is evidence which places him in Greece at an even earlier age. There is also evidence that the Chinese may be the inventors of the shadow show (VB).*

ity of indirect expression gave the puppeteer the opportunity to spread political and religious ideas. We know, for example, that Buddhist priests, in preaching their creed in Japan, presented religious scenes of Buddha's life with marionettes. The puppet show has also been used for political ends. The marionette theater was used by the Chinese revolutionaries to spread their Communist ideas. Even today, puppets are used in India to induce the people to practice family planning and achieve other government objectives. The puppet show's inherent freedom for improvisation permits reference to everyday facts and events, and puppets have often represented a sole courageous political opposition. The puppeteer, for this reason, has at times been persecuted by the authorities, religious as well as political.

The puppeteer's characters have also been persecuted with him. Kasper, Pulcinella, Punch, Guignol, Petrouchka, Jan Klaasen, Karagöz, and others have endured, in the course of their history, both triumphs and persecutions. Today things are better for them.

In the West, through new artistic forms, the puppet show has been revived. Sophie Taeuber-Arp, Paul Klee, Bernard Luginbühl, and Harry Kramer are just a few representatives of the kinetic art trying to create new puppets; puppeteers in the East and West, including the U.S.A., see a new possibility of growth in their advanced art. The modern theater has also accepted puppets. Good examples are the Marionetteteatern of Michael Mesches in Stockholm, or the successful presentation of the revolutionary script "1789" at the Théâtre du Soleil in Paris, in which, as in the old "mysteries," actors and puppets share the scenes. As in any new form of art, this could remain at the experimental level, but in the best of cases it can be classified as art. It is possible that a revival such as that of the Bread and Puppet Theater in New York City might mean new directions. This has become street theater with presentations in supermarkets, churches, gyms, and schools, and on crowded street corners. Its public

8

The Opera dei Pupi in Sicily. The scene represents the battle of Roncesvalles, Spain, where in 778 the rear guard of Charlemagne was ambushed by the Saracens and defeated. According to the legend, Roland, the most trusted of Charlemagne's twelve paladins, was killed. Today the repertoire of the Sicilian puppet theater still includes this epic, which was spread here by minstrels during the Norman and French occupation. Marionettes first arrived in Sicily from Naples during the nineteenth century. They are still presented in the traditional fashion in theaters around the island. Marionettes fifty-five inches tall, dressed in rich costumes and armor created with artistic skill, highlight these shows (PM).

consists of people from every walk of life. With this kind of public, it is easy for their participation to become part of the set. From these improvised settings follows an orderly presentation of scenes and pictures.

In Asia the shadow and puppet shows, still in the traditional state, can continue to survive, thanks to the strong traditional attachments of its people. In many countries, such as China, Indonesia, and Thailand, the shows are receiving government subsidies.

In Eastern Europe, particularly Czechoslovakia, Russia, and Rumania, as well as in the German Democratic Republic, the puppet show is an integral part of every kindergarten and every school. It is an interesting question as to why the West hasn't applied this technique as a new way of learning in the school systems, since it promotes the arts of speaking, poetry, sculpture, painting, and music in equal measure.

It is time to mention and thank those Swiss, German, and Austrian puppet-show pioneers of the past and present. Homage must be given to Count Franz Pocci, Josef Leonhard (Papa) Schmid, Anton Aicher, Helmut Scherrer, Richard Teschner, Max Jakob, Marcelle Monyer, René Morax, Alfred Altherr, Jakob Flach, and many others who have searched in their own way for new forms. Also to be mentioned are many Italians, French, Belgians, Dutch, English, Americans, Scandinavians, Russians, Czechoslovakians, and Rumanians. They are, however, not the only innovators or performers whom we should thank. Hundreds and thousands of other puppeteers, mostly poor vagrants, and sometimes persecuted by the authorities, have contributed to preserving the art. They have rescued it through the centuries and brought it to our own age. Their names are not to be found in any history book, but rather in some governmental files and court minutes. Although they have generally been forgotten, some have been rescued through literature, such as Master Pedro in Cervantes' *Don Quixote* and the puppeteer Tendler in Theodor Storm's *Pole Puppenspieler*. They are to be recognized as representatives of the thousands and thousands of unknown puppeteers who have preserved and advanced the art. To all of them, this book is dedicated.

The True Puppet Show

The oldest paintings north of the Alps of a true puppet show are to be found in the Bodleian Library of Oxford. They are two miniatures in one manuscript, "Li romans du boin roi Alixandre," painted in 1344 by Johan de Grise. In one illustration there is a character with a hooked nose and a cudgel, together with a woman; in the other are two armed characters with cudgels or swords, perhaps symbolizing two knights. What are they doing? They are fighting. They are thus performing the act that has been the theme of puppet shows in every country: the quarrel, the fight, and the beating. In one illustration we see three children seated in front of the puppets' glass. We can imagine that they are madly enjoying the presentation. Since Harlequin (Arlecchino), Kasper, Punch, Guignol and their predecessors, puppet shows have been loved not only by children but also by those adults who know

that a beating is good when others get it. They admire the actions of those cunning, ill-bred fellows who for centuries have beaten up Death, the Devil, emperors, kings, clergymen, robbers, dragons, enraged dogs, witches, and policemen whenever these unfortunates happened to cross their paths. They themselves are bravely kicked and punched, but they always find their way out of even the most entangled situations.

It is still maintained that among the ancestors of these impertinent, quarrelsome fellows, the court jester was the unfortunate one forced to pay with beatings for the freedom of speech they enjoyed. Others are said to descend from Karagöz, the foulmouthed Turkish-Islamic comedian who moved to Europe with the gypsies or followed the returning Crusaders. Among them, it is not difficult to recognize the Italian puppet Pulcinella and his grand-

Early documentation of a puppet show: miniature by Johan de Grise, 1344.

11

*Kasper's friends and enemies. Above (left to right):
the good King, a Nobleman (PM), the Devil (ML), another
nobleman. Below (left to right): the good Blacksmith,
the Policeman, the gracious Gretel, the Witch (PM).*

Kasper's friends are the children, or even those adults
who understand children's logic. For example, when the
owner of the house in which Kasper lives goes to ask for
payment of the rent, the unlucky Kasper has no money.
This is because he has had no work, because of his
drunkenness, and because he gave away or lost the money
which he earned by begging or trickery. Therefore, the
landlord's claims are totally silly. And, since no argument
serves the purpose, he is beaten up. Kasper wins because
the owner is—in children's logic—wrong. However, it is
incomprehensible that a child's cruelty would extend as
far as tricking disabled and old people, as does Kasper
and all the other puppets. Kasper, Guignol, Punch,
Petrouchka, Jan Klaasen, and all the other cruel, immoral

characters of the puppet shows, such as the Devil, the Witch, Death, and the Ghost—are they bad company for the children? What about the jealous queen who has Snow White murdered and wants to eat her heart and her liver? And what about Grimm's fable "The Devil with the Three Golden Hairs," in which the stupid hero conquers the princess and her kingdom with his amoral tricks? Never mind. The imaginative form given to the fable and the puppet show stimulates the child's imagination. The child requires clear facts presented with strong colors, because he cannot master complex circumstances and ambiguous facts, such as occur in real life. This is the reason that many comic strips and cartoons become successful. One must use fast transitions instead of a slow evolution; simple contrasts rather than subtle gradations: rich versus poor, old versus young, good versus bad.

Figures of an English paper theater of the nineteenth century.

14

father Maccus, the Greco-Roman clown. The representations of the original Pulcinella, Punch, Polichinelle, Kasper, and their relatives give something of everything. Even the peasant, mocked for his insensibility, becomes famous for his artfulness and ingenuity. It all depends on the puppeteer's ability to satisfy the people's wants and preferences.

Since the puppet show—as no other dramatic production—exists for the pure pleasure of the audience, its directness immediately succeeds in reaching the spectators. Moreover, it can be presented everywhere and without preparation. All that is needed for its simple means of expression is a cloth laid on the hand or an old glove with two painted eyes, or simply a painted face on a fingernail, or Ping-Pong balls placed on the fingers as characters.

Sergei Obraszov, the famous Russian puppet showman, director of the Central Theater in Moscow, tells us in his book *The Puppeteer's Trade*[5] of a puppet consisting of a sock slipped over one's hand that represented a black baby. "The curled hair was made from scraps of astrakhan. The white eyes were standing out vertically, the black pupils made from shiny buttons of children's shoes. The checkered dressing gown was made from an old jacket." Truly this is not a new idea; a mother knows well that, from some remnants, it is always possible to make dolls for her baby. But Obraszov, with that very simple puppet, succeeded in awakening the public interest and in creating a new expressive form. Describing another puppet (a fist covered at first with a cloth and later concealed with a sock), Obraszov says all he had to do was to "let the index finger stand slightly out to create a nose, then extend my ring finger slightly below for a chin. By moving the other fingers, the face was animated; the creased sock became a wrinkled face, giving a comical effect. The only embellishments needed were two buttons sown to the sock to form the eyes, a pair of eyeglasses, and two lines representing the mouth. As a result, the face was extremely vivid and expressive, limited only by my ability to move my hand."

What is needed in the true puppet show? A head carved or formed with any kind of substance, placed on the index finger; a cloth to hide the hand, with two lateral holes or two sleeves in which the thumb and the little finger (or even the middle finger) are placed. The second hand is left free to manipulate another figure in the same way. Moreover, the puppet show is the only dramatic show in which the dialogue is guided by the spectators. Their interruptions motivate the actions and thus become a part of it. "Are you all here?" asks Gioppino. "Yes! Yes!" the children shout. A good puppet showman can, at this point, obtain audience participation through the use of some very simple ploys. Robert Adolf Stemmle[6] tells us of Hans Deppe, a practitioner of the art of participation and an excellent puppeteer. One of his puppet shows was performed in a mining locality for almost five hundred miners' children. They saw "Antrascek and Juracek," or "The Robbers in Siebenbürgen." Children and young girls watched breathlessly as Kasper met Gretel, the miller's daughter, and immediately decided to marry her. When Kasper left to follow the brigands, the children had to take good care of Gretel. When the bad brigand Juracek came in and saw Gretel, the only thing left for him to do was to fall in love. But the spectators started to shout: "She is Kasper's fiancée! Leave her in peace!"

Juracek amused himself in provoking them: "What do you want? Don't you have anything to say; otherwise I'll start losing my temper and I'll throw all of you out. If Gretel is not willing, then I am going to rape her!" He had already started to pull Gretel's braids. The children would not move, frightened and perspiring. Then a little boy, perhaps not even eight years old, stepped up to the front of the stage and yelled with a threatening and clear voice: "You leave her alone!" "Oh, oh," the brigand laughed disdainfully, "what do you want, you little thing?" The brigand grabbed Gretel, trying to escape with her in the dark forest. But he did not succeed. The little boy pulled out a wooden shoe, aimed and threw it, and hit him. This gave

15

the signal. All the other children, also wearing wooden shoes, started to throw them. From a total of five hundred children, there were one thousand possible strikes.

Says Stemmle, "Hans Deppe and I were lying on the theater floor with sacks and luggage on our heads to let that dramatic flood of people pass, leaving us uninjured. Then we shook hands and looked at each other in fright. That was the last time we would experience such a dangerous theatrical presentation."

The immediate and touching effectiveness of a puppet performance and its simple technique made it a natural for wandering minstrels. The poem "The Runner" by Hugo von Trimberg, written in 1300, is about comedians who pulled the puppets out of their coats and made all the bystanders laugh with their jokes. The puppet theaters of minstrels met the liking of the public that used to patronize the marketplace: crude with simple ropes, based on sex, criticizing the customs of society. The minstrel was one of the few persons who brought news of the world into the towns, villages, inns, and even the most remote farmhouses. And he also knew how to speak to the people, and could give the uneducated audience the knowledge of a richer life.

In fact, wasn't he also carrier and mediator of an old science that was manifest in magic tricks, fortune telling, and prodigious remedies? Wasn't he himself an offspring of the oldest and most mysterious family of the gypsies? His puppets were not merely entertainment but had something of a magical importance. In southern Germany, it was noted as late as the twentieth century that the Kaspers of two different theaters, independently of each other, had on their foreheads a "wart" [7] that was a particular sign of the demigods and divinity of India, as they appear in the puppet theater and in the arts of that faraway country—a sign that alludes to their "third eye," the sign of a "magic" [8] faculty.

Thus, the puppet of the minstrel—made in his own image—was simultaneously clown, critic of reality, and announcer of a desired more beautiful

A comedian-magician attracting customers with a puppet. From a magic book of the fairs, Hoccius Doccius, *of the eighteenth century.*

world. Loved and admired by the people, he brought happiness to the children and the simple-minded. He was a prophet for the poor and oppressed, rich in the clown's freedom; he was a rebel, who, at least in the show, could do things no other could dare. This explains the hostility of the church and persecution by the authorities to which the puppeteer was exposed for centuries.

We do not know how the medieval puppeteer looked. The puppets that he had must have included, in addition to local characters and a clown, at least the Clergyman, the Devil, Death, the King, the Princess or a Good Fairy, and a Policeman or similar representative of local authority. Later on, exotic elements were added to this group of typical puppets: the Crocodile, Turks, and Negroes. Unlike the various local Italian characters, the French Polichinelle and Guignol, and the English Punch, Kasper never had his own unique characterization. Frisch,[9] in his dictionary of 1741, describes the direct predecessors of Kasper, Meister Hämmerlein and Pickelhering (herring), as having horrible faces. We also know that the Dutch puppeteers in the seventeenth and eighteenth centuries traveled through Germany and Switzerland with their clown Jan Klaasen, who was very successful. He presented himself as a jovial good man with a large red nose and hunched back. He resembled Kasper somewhat, but his characteristics were more those of the town fool and the presumptuous braggart, just like the comedian type of the popular theater, with whose characters he undoubtedly had something in common.

A study made in 1931 [10] by a German puppeteer to determine the appearance of Kasper resulted in many diverse conceptions. The typical Kasper, with a hooked nose, a pointed chin, and a smiling thin face, has been presented in the German puppet theater as a cunning hero, handy with a cudgel, who always defeats all of his rivals. It has been argued that this is not the true Kasper, that Kasper cannot be identified in a particular way. Every puppeteer gave his puppet a particular expression according to his personal experience. Some puppeteers, for example, saw in Kasper the clown with a constantly running nose and a mouth full of laughter. He was always ready to exaggerate to the extreme with vulgar talk. He had an energetic chin and semiclosed eyes. Other impressions were, just to mention some, those of a little man, well fed, with the smiling face of a rascal. Kasper also had the well-known features of a flat nose in the middle of a serene, small face and a head round like a ball. This last characterization appears to be a way of discrediting the original vigorous and rude nature of the puppet. In this incarnation his clean clothes are well matched. Even though they are mended, it looks more like they have been decorated. His appearance is graceful, as graceful and empty as his comedies. While the children get bored, this Kasper is loved among more sophisticated circles, who see in the old Kasper and his foul jokes a bad influence on the young. This is why they have accepted Kasper as a helpful, good boy. They even let him give advice on how to clean teeth and how to put some money in the savings account each week.

But wait—soon the old Kasper will reappear and will beat in the heads of those sophisticated, well-to-do people until they lose their senses. And with a violent kick in the behind he will send them to the most infernal Hell. And the children will laugh again just like the Italian children with their Gioppino and the French with their Guignol.

Opening vignette of Kasper in Turkey *by Count Franz Pocci.*

The English "Punch"

This is how two groups of scholars, which we shall call Puff and Paff, dispute his origin:

PUFF: Punch arrived in England in 1662, during the celebration of the Restoration.

PUFF: Punch arrived from France. He was the younger brother of the insolent and arrogant Polichinelle, a malicious caricature of good King Henry IV of France.

PUFF: In England he was first called Punchinello

17

Kasper in conversation with the castle guard. In the following scene he will cheat the gullible fool. At all times, this cheerful character of the puppet theater can achieve his goal with insolence, peasant cunning, or strength. To satisfy his whims, he doesn't stop at anything (PM).

and was described by some reporters as a boasting fencer and battler with a strident voice and vulgar sense of humor.

PAFF: Punch is a variation of Pulcinella, a well-known and entertaining figure of the puppet theater since the Elizabethan period (1558–1603).

PAFF: He can be traced back in England. With his hunched back and his big nose he is a close relative of the Pulcinella of the *commedia dell'arte*.

PAFF: At the beginning of the eighteenth century he was so popular that he took part in all the puppet shows, including the mysteries.

PAFF: In the eighteenth century, when puppets were removed from the regular theater, he became a true puppet and developed his own characteristics. This is how it has been reported by others.[11]

PUFF-PAFF: Punch becomes the beloved of the public in streets and at fairs. He wears the characteristic red and yellow costume of the English clowns and carries the slapstick of the court jester. Always accompanied by his dog Toby.

PUFF-PAFF: After a time he marries Judy, who brings to the scene a great number of friends and acquaintances: [12] These include:

The Doctor: Found in every Punch and Judy show.

The Waiter: One of the oldest characters, a black, now named Jim Crow.

The Blind Man: He has the appearance of a rascal and is treated as such by Punch. On this point, all the scholars agree.

Pretty Polly: The pretty girl friend of Punch, to the displeasure of Judy. Polly is not a puppet in the real sense, but because of her slim figure she is activated by a rod.

Jack Catch, the Hangman: He appears in all the shows.

The Constable and the Officer: They represent law and order. At times they are used as gravediggers.

The Devil: A dangerous type, but deep down a fool. Colored red and black.

Scaramuccia: Once a popular surprise character of the puppet theater, who had been influenced by some Italian characters. He became a close friend of the Punch family.

Hector: The stallion. He appears from time to time. Lately he has been replaced by a car.

Baby: Pride of his parents, Punch and Judy. Punch is particularly happy that he looks like him.

The Court Clerk: A surprise puppet. He is used for unusual parts, especially when a special effect which lends itself to his stretchable neck is needed.

Against such an invasion of friends and enemies (and against the competition of other marionettes) Punch, alone, defends himself furiously. Even Judy gets her share. The clown's slapstick becomes a very solid instrument. Distributing beatings which would make even the very strong Kasper or the most beastly Guignol jealous, Punch maintains his leading position.

Only he has the exclusive use of the puppeteer's right hand. Judy and all the rest have to share the left hand. The English animator of Punch and Judy, like his own hero, always works by himself. An assistant helps him carry his small theater, which is easy to set up; attracts people with a horn, bagpipe, or drum; and collects the money. Only during the summer, on English beaches, do the typical vagrant theaters of Punch and Judy exist. Today in London

Punch of England and the Devil of France. When puppets knock heads together, there is no language barrier. Until the end of the nineteenth century, the vagrant puppeteer was a part of fairs and religious observances. Italian, German, Dutch, French, Austrian, English, and Czech puppeteers toured all of Europe, always attracting big audiences (PM).

20

there are no more than four. As in the case of the Italian puppeteers, the greatest part of the texts have been transmitted orally. Only very few Punch and Judy comedies have been written or printed since 1825. The famous travel author Prince Hermann Pückler-Muskau [13] noted in one of his letters a classical presentation of Punch and Judy that was shown daily in the streets of London at the beginning of the last century. This presentation is summarized here, accompanied by the drawings of George Cruikshank.

As the curtain goes up, Punch is singing "Marlborough Goes to War." Then he appears dancing and in good humor, and tells the spectators his thoughts with funny lines. He introduces himself as a cheerful type, a lover of jokes. He claims that he does not understand much of anything else and that he is moved only by the gentle sex. He spends his money at will and his only purpose is to live, laugh, and become as fat as possible.

After this monologue, he turns around and calls Judy, who doesn't pay any attention to him, and instead sends him her dog.

Punch caresses and teases the dog. The dog bites his nose and pulls him by the pants until, after a funny scuffle, Punch stops him and punishes him severely. During this noisy episode, Scaramuccia enters the scene carrying a big cane. He asks Punch why he is beating a dog which is very dear to Judy, a dog who never bites anyone. "Even I never beat up a dog."

Punch answers, "But my dear Scaramuccia, what do you have in your hands?" "Oh, nothing other than a violin; do you want to hear how it plays? Come here and listen to this magnificent instrument!" "Thanks, thanks, dear Scaramuccia," says Punch modestly, "I can well distinguish the sound from afar." Scaramuccia, however, doesn't give up, and while dancing, swinging his cane, and singing, all of a sudden he hits Punch on the head, who

22

makes believe he doesn't notice it. Punch starts dancing and, taking advantage of it, takes away the cane
from Scaramuccia; twice he hits Scaramuccia so hard
on the head that it falls off at their feet.

Where Punch hits, no more grass grows. "Ha,
ha," he says, "did you hear the violin, my dear
Scaramucchia? What a beautiful sound it makes!
But where is Judy? Why don't you come, my dear
Judy?"

In the meantime, Punch hides the body of Scaramuccia behind the curtain. When Judy appears,
she reveals herself to be the feminine version of her
husband, with a similar hunchback and a nose even
worse than his. A loving scene follows, full of jokes,
after which Punch asks for the baby. Judy goes to
get him, while Punch, in a second monologue,
brags about his fortune as a husband and father.
As soon as the little monster arrives, both parents,
ecstatic with joy, caress him tenderly, calling him
by the most affectionate names. Judy leaves to at-

tend to her domestic chores, leaving the infant in the arms of the father, who, even though inexperienced as a nanny, plays with the child. The child, however, starts to cry at the top of his lungs and becomes naughty. At first Punch tries to calm him down, but soon loses his temper and starts to beat him up. Since the child starts to cry even louder and wets in Punch's arms, Punch becomes furious. Cursing, he throws him out of the window right into the middle of the street, where, among all the spectators, the child breaks his neck. Punch leans out of the stage, clowning, shakes his head, and starts to laugh, dance, and sing:

> Sleep, oh my baby, the baby is dead,
> You dirty pig, go away from home.
> Soon I will buy another one, it is not difficult,
> From the same place he came, others will come.

At that moment Judy reenters and, preoccupied, asks for her "darling." "The baby went to sleep," answers Punch calmly. In the end, however, he has to confess that while he was playing with the baby, he fell out of the window. Judy is beside herself with grief. She pulls her hair and calls her terrible tyrant the worst names. To no avail, he promises her that he will buy another beautiful baby. She doesn't listen to reason and leaves, crying out terrible threats. Punch cannot stop laughing. Dancing very boldly, he hits his head against the walls. Judy in the meantime reenters and comes up behind him with a broomstick in her hand. She starts hitting him with all her strength. At first Punch tries to calm her down, telling her that he would never throw the baby out of the window again. He begs her not to take this joke so hard. But, seeing that nothing will help, he again loses his patience and proceeds, as with Scaramuccia, to beat the hell out of poor Judy. "Well," he says very cordially, "our fight has finished, my dear. If you are happy, so am I. Come on, get up, sweet Judy. What, you don't want to? Then down you go, too!" And she is thrown from the window, like her baby.

In the second act we see Punch during a meeting with his girl friend Polly, whom he treats poorly. He assures her that only she can distract him from his anxieties and that if he had all of the wise Solomon's wives at his disposal, he would kill them all for her love. Later another suitor and friend of Polly comes along. This time Punch doesn't kill him. He is satisfied just to mock him. Then Punch declares that he wants to take advantage of the good weather to go horseback riding. The horse he happens to end up with is a very fiery stallion. For a while Punch tries to remain on his back, but after many ridiculous maneuvers he is thrown on the ground by the recalcitrant and untamable animal. He calls for help, and luckily his friend the Doctor, who is passing by, promptly runs to his aid. Punch lies on the ground, half dead and in terrible pain. The Doctor tries to calm him down, takes his pulse, and asks him, "Where were you wounded? Is it here?" "No, a little lower." "On your chest?" "No, a little lower." "Oh, did you break your leg?" "No,

a little higher." "But, then, where?" At this point Punch hits the Doctor very hard in a certain part of the body, jumps up laughing, and dances as he sings:

> This is where I am wounded
> And now, thanks to the sympathy, I am well.
> I only fell down on the green grass.
> Do you, jackass, believe I am made of glass?

Without saying a word, the Doctor leaves furiously. Soon afterward he returns with his big cane, saying, "Here, dear Punch, I bring you some very healthful medicine, which is good only for you," and starts to beat Punch's back with the cane. "Thanks a million," he yells, "but I am already well. I cannot stand medicine, it gives me pain in the stomach and the hips. . . ." "That is only because you have taken too small a dose," the Doctor interrupts. "Take a little more and you will surely feel better." Punch replies: "You doctors all talk the same way. Why don't you try it yourself?" "We

26

Punch and his wife, Judy, who at first was called Joan (PM).

never take our own medicine," the Doctor says. "You, however, still need an additional dose."

Punch appears defeated, falls down exhausted, and begs forgiveness. When the gullible Doctor leans toward him, he very suddenly jumps on him. After a brief fight he takes the cane away from him and proceeds as usual. "Now you must try a little of your own new medicine, my dearest Doctor, only a tiny bit, dear friend. Take that! And that!"

"Oh, my God, he is killing me!" cries the Doctor. "Doctors always die when they take their own medicine," says Punch. "Be patient—here, just one more pill." He sticks the cane into the Doctor's stomach. "Do you feel the beneficial effects inside you?" The Doctor falls down dead.

After many incidents, all with the same tragic result, the police finally send the Constable to arrest Punch. He finds him, as usual, in a very good humor, busy, playing with a big bell. Their dialogue is concise:

CONSTABLE: Mr. Punch, put aside the music and the songs, I come here to shut your mouth forever.

PUNCH: Who the hell are you?

CONSTABLE: Don't you recognize me?

PUNCH: Not a chance, and I don't care to know you.

CONSTABLE: Oh, but you have no choice. I am the Constable.

PUNCH: Go, I don't need you. I am capable of taking care of my own affairs. Thanks a million, but I don't need a constable.

CONSTABLE: It's all right—in this case the Constable needs you.

PUNCH: What the hell! And what for, if I may ask?

CONSTABLE: Oh, only to hang you. You have killed Scaramuccia, your wife and your son, the Doctor....

PUNCH: Oh, hell! What's it to you? If you stay a little longer, you'll end up like the others.

CONSTABLE: Don't fool around! You are a murderer, and this is the warrant for your arrest.

PUNCH: And I also have a warrant to give you immediately.

Punch grabs the bell which until that moment he had kept behind his back and strikes the Constable's chin with such force that he, like his predecessors, falls to the floor, dead. Soon after this he does a somersault and runs away. From backstage he is heard happily singing:

> The jug goes to fetch the water
> Until it breaks.
> A cheerful generous man
> Could not care less.

The Court Clerk also comes into contact with Punch and meets the same fate. Lastly, the Hangman himself goes out to get Punch, who runs into him accidentally. In meeting him for the first time, Punch appears confused. He gives up and tries to flatter Mr. Catch, calling him "old friend" and asking him how Mrs. Catch is feeling. The Hangman, how-ever, makes him understand that their friendship is over and reminds him that he is a criminal who has killed many people, including his own wife and child. "As far as those two murders are concerned," Punch defends himself, "they were my property and everyone is free to dispose of his own belongings as he pleases." "And why did you kill the poor Doctor who came to help you?" "Only in self defense, dear Mr. Catch, because his medicine was killing me." All of these excuses don't help. With the help of three or four henchmen, Catch ties him up and takes him to prison.

In the following act, at the back of the stage, we see Punch behind bars. He is very upset and dis-couraged but nevertheless tries to kill time in his own way by singing a song. Catch enters the scene and, with the help of two assistants, prepares the gallows in front of the prison. Punch cries, not in remorse but because he misses his Polly. Soon, how-ever, he gathers his courage and begins to joke about

29

the gallows, comparing it to a beautiful tree that has been planted to improve the scene. "How beautiful it will look," he cries out, "when it blooms!" Then some men bring in a coffin and place it at the foot of the gallows.

"What is the meaning of this?" asks Punch. . . . "Ah, without doubt it must be the basket in which we will put the fruit." In the meantime Catch enters, greets Punch, opens the cell, and makes him understand that since everything is ready he can come out if he likes. It is easy to understand why Punch is in no hurry to come out. After a long discussion, Catch loses his cool and cries out, "There is no help now. You have to come out to be hanged."

PUNCH: You wouldn't be so cruel!
CATCH: Why were you so cruel as to kill your wife and child?
PUNCH: Only for that you are going to be cruel to me and kill me?

Catch grabs him by the hair and pulls him out of the cell. Punch asks forgiveness and promises he will change. "Now, my dear Punch," says Catch fearlessly, "be so kind as to put your head in the rope and soon everything will be over." Punch makes believe that he doesn't know how and puts his head in the rope the wrong way. "My God, how awkward you are!" cries Catch. "This is the way you put your head through"—he shows him. "And is this the way to pull the rope?" yells Punch, who at the same time pushes the careless hangman, killing him. Punch runs to hide behind a wall. Two men arrive to carry the body away, and believing that it is the criminal who died, they put the body in the coffin and carry it out.

The best is yet to come for Punch, since now the Devil himself comes to take him away. In vain Punch argues that the Devil mustn't be very smart to want to take his best friend on earth. The Devil doesn't want to hear any excuses, and reaches out

30

toward Punch with his long, horrible hands. Punch, however, is not easily scared. To defend his own skin, he reaches for his deadly stick. A terrible fight ensues. Who would have expected this? Punch, who has been near death, remains at the end the happy victor. He picks up the black Devil, and carrying him around as a trophy, laughs and sings:

> Hurrah! Punch, the misery is over,
> The Devil is dead, hurrah!

Friends from France

C'est guignolant!—"What a clown!" People in Lyon rapturously applauded the puppeteer Laurent Mourguet in his new theater, Caveau des Célestins, located in the basement of a cafe. Mourguet was happy. Finally he had a permanent place for his theater. For more than thirty years he had been working with his puppets at a small park called the Chinese Garden during the summer and at his home on Place Saint-Paul during the winter. He performed for children. However, he preferred to perform for workers, carftsmen, and simple people like himself. A silk weaver by profession, he had lived through all the crises that the industry is continually exposed to.

To escape this permanent misery, Mourguet decided in 1793 to become a tooth puller, and he practiced in the marketplaces. In this job he made some money because he was able to attract clients with the help of a little puppet he called Polichinelle. After ten years Mourguet became a professional puppeteer and a partner with Père Thomas, who played the violin and sang songs of his own composition during intermission. Later Thomas also made a puppet with the features of a soap maker who is eternally thirsty, with a red nose and a crooked mouth. The puppet was called Gnafron. Some historians believe that Gnafron was created after Guignol. In any case, about 1810 Mourguet bought the puppet called Girolamo from a silk weaver in the town of Chignolo. Girolamo is the smart fool of Milanese marionettes. Mourguet welcomed him into his puppet group. He would be altered. He would have the large face and the somewhat strident voice of his owner, thus assuming the character of a Lyonese silk weaver. It is possible that Girolamo from Chignolo became Guignol.

The puppet historian Maindron is not of the same opinion as to Guignol's origins. To substantiate his argument, he refers to research made on the puppet theater in Lyon, published around 1865 by Janis-Louis Onofrio. According to this study,

31

Mourguet named his puppet after a favorite expression of one of his habitual spectators, who, at the funniest moments, would shout, *C'est guignolant!* The question remains, did this word exist before Guignol? Also, the words *guigne* and *guignon* ("misfortune") come into the discussion, since Guignol was created as an unlucky character.[14] According to a more recent theory the name was taken from a comedy of Dorvigny, *Nitouche et Guignolet*, presented in Lyon in 1804. The main character, Guignolet, is a little peasant who at times is naive and at times is smart.[15]

But what is the purpose of disputing the origin of the word? Guignol is already a Lyonese silk weaver and is wearing the costume of the *canuts* (name given to the silk weavers of Lyon in 1800). His costume consists of a black hat showing only a small plait of hair (commonly known as the mouse tail) and a dark brown wool jacket up to his neck and down to his knees. His comedies represent the daily life of workers and craftsmen. He knows well the presumptions and the rudeness of the bourgeoisie and takes the side of the weak who try to defend themselves against those who take advantage of them. "In this fight the arms used are satirical and the beatings are only with a stick. It is always certain that Guignol will be involved in some crisis." [16]

In France, Guignol has given his name to all the true puppet theaters. Texts conceived by his creator and written down by friends during performances were published during the life of Mourquet, who died in 1844. We find an important bibliography of Guignol comedies in the appendix of the book published by Andre Charles Gervais.[17]

Guignol is an incorrigible optimist and often naive. But he fights openly and fearlessly with his stick when his rights or the rights of others are at stake. The fights mostly begin as a result of the daily financial miseries which he and his world endure. Often Guignol tries to drown his rage and misfortunes in wine, making his situation even worse. But he gets new courage to go on living and to vindicate himself against his enemies. In "Les frères Coq," he finds himself in a typical unhappy situation. His brother, a stingy, rich man, has refused him a loan that is indispensable for survival. Guignol sends his son Louis to buy wine. His son lets him know that there is no money in the house. "Ah, don't you have any money? Take this, exchange it!" yells Guignol, and with desperate rage he slaps his son in the face. Louis, saddened, answers, "Dad, why do you hit me? It is not my fault that you don't have any money and you are mad!" "You are right, I am a fool!" Guignol apologizes. Remembering his brother with a stone heart, he says, "Yes, he is the wicked one and my misfortune!" Then, addressing his thoughts to his brother: "It is your fault that I hit Louis; one day you will pay for it!"

Guignol, round-faced, flat-nosed, and with triangular eyebrows, gave his name to the true French puppet theater.

32

Gnafron was a character used for the first time in 1800 by Père Thomas, a Lyonese puppeteer, in a new act by Gaston Baty, a French promoter of the puppet show. He made the drunkard, to which Gnafron over the course of the centuries has been reduced, a companion who is always thirsty and loudmouthed, but a true friend of the famous Guignol whom Laurent Mourguet of Lyon gave to the world of puppets (ML).

Guignol always portrays the characteristics of the local environment. This can also be said for the other characters associated with him: his wife, Madelon; his boss, the silk maker Battandier; Canezou, the greedy landlord; Cadet, a young man who doesn't err in the direction of too much intelligence. Later on, in Paris, Guignol's family increases with another son, Guillaume. Gnafron is a good and inseparable friend to Guignol, kind but a bit morose. It can be understood how the Guignol character, independent and insensitive to all intimidation, was a source of unrest for the authorities. During the reign of Napoleon III, the animators of Guignol were obliged, in a sort of self-censorship, to write down the texts before presentations and follow them carefully. For the proper puppet theater this was deadly interference, since that institution's strength lay in its ability to improvise.

In Paris, where Guignol had been known since 1818, his unique character was generalized. "Only the external figure survived." [18] In the years between the World Wars, with his opinions stranded, the chauvinist Guignol became a small civilian, noisy and dissatisfied, constantly in conflict with the police. And today, on the Champs-Élysées, in the Luxembourg Gardens, and in some marketplaces in Parisian suburbs, we encounter theater with Guignol as the main character. In Lyon there are still two theaters which present daily shows for children and tourists. We must also mention the many associations which are trying to revive Guignol in the spirit of his creator, Laurent Mourguet.

The Marionette Show

The rich Callia gave a dinner in 422 B.C. And, since he loved to show off his wealth, he made sure that an elaborately set table, abundant wine, and beautiful women would not be missing. But the big attraction of the evening was the presentation of a pantomime by a traveling comedian of Syracuse and a puppet theater.

Puppets and theatrical presentations were in fashion among the Greeks, or so it has been written by the Greek and Roman authors. For many, the puppet theater was the symbol of human destiny. Plato compares man to a marionette, manipulated by the hand of the gods according to their passions. Aristotle imagines the God of the Universe to be just like a puppeteer who moves men as though they were puppets. Horatio, the satirist Persio Flacco, and the Roman emperor Marcus Aurelius doubt the free will of man, since they compare him to marionettes. The Greek marionettes—*agálmata neurospasta* ("moving images")—were made of painted terra cotta, wax, ivory, or wood. The exceptionally well made ones were also made of silver. Similar to puppets still in use in Sicily and Liège, they hung from a steel bar which was attached to the head. Their arms and legs may have been activated by strings. It should be noted that the Greek as well as the Indian marionettists came to be known as neurospastes, or string pullers.

The satirist-philosopher Apuleius, author of *The Golden Ass,* in his literary work *De Mundo* compliments the perfection of the Roman marionettes. "When those who direct the movements of these wooden human figures pull the face string, the chin will turn, the head will ascend, the eyes will turn, the hands will be ready to help, and the entire figure

Ulysses refuses the magic potion of Circe. Doric comedy of about 300 B.C. The "buffoon" of that time wore a pillow on his stomach and back as well as a mask on his face.

35

Ludus monstrorum.

In ludo monstror designat uanita vanitat

The first known presentation of a puppet show was shown in the manuscript "Hortus deliciarum," written by the abbess Herrad von Landsberg (1170). The technique of the show is perhaps similar to that of the marionettes aux genoux as described earlier.

will seem graciously animated." The Romans had many names for the marionettes: *pupae, sigillae, sigilliolae, imagunculae, homunculi.*

The first evidence of marionettes in Germany came in the late Middle Ages. At the beginning, the repertoire must have consisted of chivalrous fights and reenactments of old German legends. One of the few existing sources on this subject, a drawing in an encyclopedia of 1170, written by Herrad von Landsberg, shows two knights dueling with swords and shields and leads us to the conclusion that they were activated by two horizontal ropes pulled by two hidden persons.[19]

Also belonging to the repertoire were the numerous holy presentations taken from the mysteries of the late medieval era, in which the puppets often recited together with the audience. In that period, the strange word *Himmelreich* ("the Kingdom of Heaven") appears to designate the puppet theater and the puppeteer. In one document of the Council of Basil, the following is recorded: "In August of

1450, a betrothed paid five Plapperts, while the director of a *Himmelreich* paid just one." We can agree with some scholars who are of the opinion that the name *Himmelreich* came from the holy presentations performed by the puppeteers of the time. Nevertheless, it is not impossible that this denotation was due to the fact that the puppets were "pulled from the top and often lowered down almost as if arriving from the sky." [20]

Until the seventeenth century, we have little information about the puppet theater. The only reliable sources concerning the growth of this popular amusement are the old council documents of the municipal and local archives, from which we can unearth the names and origins of various puppeteers and come to a conclusion as to the character of the comedies presented: "Nördlingen 1582: Balthasar Klein of St. Joachimstal" asks permission to present "two beautiful stories from the Old Testament, to be recited like comedies with beautiful figures."

In 1583, in Augsburg, Caspar Schuechmann of

36

Polichinelle, the French character from the puppet, marionette, and live theater. He has a cynical yet serene character. He is believed to be, in spite of his relation with the Neopolitan Pulcinella, the most original French creation. For centuries Polichinelle was the main character of the French puppet and gypsy theater (ML).

Puppet theater in one of the fairs in Greenwich around 1800.

Erdtfurt (Erfurt) presented "the Passion" using artificial figures. In 1590 we read that in Tratenau (Bohemia) on Ascension Day a foreigner presented "The Last Judgement," using puppets.[21]

In the sixteenth century only one author, Hans Sachs, actually wrote for the puppet theater. Thus the spectators usually saw material more or less drawn from the puppeteer's own experiences. They also saw what the Italian, English, French, and Spanish puppet theaters presented, since in Italy, France, Spain, and England the puppet theater had been more fully developed. As early as the 1600's, at least a dozen puppet theaters were in existence in London. Puppeteers traveled all over England and gave their presentations at fairs and in the castles of the nobility. Such presentations must have strongly impressed Shakespeare. He often mentions them, and at one point Hamlet expresses the desire to perform in a puppet theater.

Very often the puppeteers were Italians who were held in great esteem in England. A commentator facing the stage explained the act, while two or more puppeteers invisibly operated behind the scenes. This method, already known in the Spanish puppet theater, and described in Cervantes' *Don Quixote*, was also practiced in other countries. Later, around

the middle of the seventeenth century, a voice was given to each figure, so that the commentator was slowly eliminated.

Reliable information about puppet presentations in France goes back only to the last quarter of the seventeenth century. It is possible that before that time the puppets of Fanchon Brioché presented on the Pont Neuf were true puppets. This conclusion has been reached because a disguised monkey, named Fagotin, took part in the presentation, and could have entangled all the control strings had there not been real puppets. Brioché, who even recited at the Royal Court before the Dauphin, created such enthusiasm among aristocratic spectators that he was invited to repeat his representation at the Court "for twenty pounds a day." [22] One of Brioché's nephews was less fortunate in one *tournée* at Soletta. The figures he presented were so lifelike that Brioché was suspected of being a witch. He saved himself only with a last-minute escape. Brioché's monkey, Fagotin, later died gloriously, stabbed by the drunken Cyrano de Bergerac, who believed him to be a juggler who mocked him for his long nose. But Fagotin had many successors. Every one of the French puppeteers had a disguised monkey and all of their monkeys were called Fago-

Hanswurst or Kasper, Kasper Larifari, Kaspar Putschenelle, etc.: the gay character in the German puppet theater. This puppet was created in a traditional form and was presented according to the puppeteer's individualism and local preferences. Contrary to the Kasper of the true puppet theater, the Hanswurst or Kasper of the marionette theater is the continuation of

the amusing and cunning Hanswurst of the popular Viennese theater, created by Josef Anton Stranitzky and Joseph Laroche. He is thus related to Arlecchino (Harlequin). The origin of Kasper is another complete discussion. The insolent and shameless Mangione (Big Eater) is a direct relative of the Indian Vidusaka, and thus the member of the Karagöz family, which includes Punch and Polichinelle (PM).

Actors and full-size marionettes in a scene from the Haymarket Theater (London, 1773).

tin. The marionette presentations, which attracted many spectators because of their magnificent costumes and scenes, were given in the Théâtre des Bamboches, founded in 1677. The construction of the theater was such that fables with dances could be presented. But this success created envy among the actors of the live threater. Actors were not only ridiculed by the puppeteers, but were also harmed by their new competition. At the end of the seventeenth century, the puppet theater was forced to move into the fairs of the Parisian suburbs. The puppeteer also had as an adversary the Church, which thought that the morality of the Parisian people was being endangered by the presentations.

From the beginning to the middle of the eighteenth century, Basel was the place for all aspiring puppeteers to go in Europe.[23] In 1695 a Burgundian named Simon du Choy wanted to present his marionette and shadow shows for the duration of the fair. In 1696 the puppeteer named Bart arrived from Bavaria. In 1697 the French puppeteer Le Rouge came from Paris. In 1698 "Stephano Landolt of Malta, according to his own description a famous puppeteer," asked permission "to perform his show for a period of time." In 1700 "André Fassel, an

Englishman, wished to show his puppets at the annual fair." He received permission but was urged to "finish his presentation by the time the evening bells play the Angelus." Almost a month later, "Hedom di Leida" asked for "an extension of an additional eight days," since he was unable to perform for "lack of instruments." His request was refused and he had to leave the city the same day. The request of puppeteer Charles Nassy from Normandy was also refused. The Venetian Clausius Semado, however, had better luck. After successful performances in Zurich, Berne, and other cities, he was given permission to perform. Carolus Leixeniz of London was also successful in procuring a permit for his company of tight-rope walkers, trapeze artists, and clowns.

In Basel these presentations were housed in different places, such as corporate facilities, rented halls, and gyms. "In Switzerland from 1670 to 1800, we can document the fact that among approximately two hundred vagrant comedians, at least sixty were puppeteers. These puppeteers were mostly Germans, Austrians, Bohemians, French, Italians, Dutchmen, and Englishmen. The German puppeteers were the first to organize themselves into corporations with a regulatory code that, among other

Paladino from the Opera dei Pupi of Acireale, one of the few marionettes of the Sicilian theater which still exists. In a manner similar to the ancient marionettes, the Sicilian marionette has a guide rod on its head. By pulling strings, even the arms can be put into motion (PP).

things, forbade them from writing down any of the text of their performances and required them to wear a uniform consisting of a black cape and hat." [24] One rarely finds requests from female puppeteers, and these are generally the wives or daughters of the directors of puppet theaters, who follow this profession more out of love than out of necessity.

In general, the puppet theater had a remarkable reputation during the eighteenth century. The few temporary restrictions and prohibitions from some authorities were the exception rather than the rule. In France the puppet theater was admitted to the Court, thanks to the Duchess of Maine, daughter of Louis XIV. Even men of culture like Le Sage and Piron wrote satirical comedies for the puppet theater. In 1746 Voltaire wrote two *couplets* (songs) for Polichinelle. In England Joseph Addison and Richard Steele, through their weekly *The Tatler,* promoted one of the best puppeteers, Martin Powell. Jonathan Swift and Henry Fielding were among the admirers of the puppet theater. For its presentation of Shakespeare's plays, Samuel Johnson seems to have preferred it to real actors. Performances were done with puppets, marionettes, and from the seventeenth century on, following the lead of Italians, with shadows. In Germany as well as England the French puppet Polichinelle, a descendant of the Italian Pulcinella, was having great success.

All the great literary works served as models for the puppet theater, and the famous puppeteer Johann Hilverding recounts that in 1702 he had even seen "operas sung by puppets" in Lüneburg. Joseph Haydn composed a series of short musical comedies for the elaborate puppet theater of Eisenstadt established by Prince Esterházy in 1766. This theater was so well thought of that Empress Maria Theresa of Austria invited it to perform at the Schönbrunn Palace near Vienna.

Like Basel, Vienna was a center of the puppet theater. Working in that theater was Joseph Anton Stranitzky (1676–1726), founder of the Wiener Volkstheater and creator of the famous peasant character

"Anfitrione," presented by the Marionette and Artists' Theater of Munich in 1924. Famous scripts always were part of the repertoire of puppet theaters. For many, their presentation was an authentic artistic endeavor, while other puppeteers wanted only to take advantage of the popularity of known texts. In that repertoire, some pathetic works were found. But some ambitious texts of interest were also uncovered, such as "Around the World in Eighty Days." Horror was also common: "The London Corpse Thieves" and "Murder in the Cellar," as well as "The Devil's Mill in the Vineyard." One puppeteer announced a spectacular presentation of the popular "Braggart Peasant of Zehnderhof," to be presented with "natural water and rain" (PM).

Hanswurst. Inspired by the model of Hanswurst, Joseph Laroche of Graz conceived his Kasper, which was received with great enthusiasm in 1769. Later Kasper became adapted to the puppet theater of Austria and southern Germany, giving its name to all the puppet theaters of that area, which became known as *Kaspertheater.* Kasper also continued as a marionette in the often-presented "Faust." Every puppeteer performed his own "Faust." Each interpretation gave the Kasper character an ever-increasing role. A good Kasper puppet could move its head, hands, and feet; maneuver a sword, slapstick, and cane; turn its eyes in a circle; stick its tongue out; and vigorously open and close its mouth. Kasper also performed during the improvised intermissions which were used by the puppeteer to embellish his comedy with some crude jokes and satirical references to the day's happenings. "Don Giovanni," like "Faust," found the public favor. Even in this drama Kasper played an important part. He also appeared, however, with somewhat less success, in

44

literary works such as "Hamlet," "Romeo and Juliet," and "Jason and Medea." In these presentations he was used for the funny parts which were not always included in the live theater. A comedy in which he appeared successfully was "Kasper Conjures Up the Devil." [25] This comedy was given with equal success by the puppet theater and the marionette theater. Written by Hans Sachs in 1551, this comedy had been adapted for the puppet theater by the end of the sixteenth century. The complete text follows:

Kasper Conjures Up the Devil

Characters:

1. The limping and hunchbacked priest (Frohbius).
2. The wandering student (Hanswurst or Kasper).
3. The peasant (Kunze).
4. The peasant woman (Rösel).

Scene: A rustic dining room.

Josef Anton Stranitzky, founder of the popular puppet theater of Vienna, in the part of Hanswurst.

SCENE 1

Frohbius and Rösel are seated in front of a table laden with food and wine.

RÖSEL: Ah, dear curate, I really don't know how to answer your questions. I can assure you that my husband and I have content and happy lives.

FROHBIUS: Yes, I believe you; however, every time I meet him he looks so depressed. That isn't very promising. He has not come to mass for a while and when I asked him about it he gave me a dirty look. He answered me very abruptly and has even forbidden me to come to his house.

RÖSEL: Alas! But you will come back, won't you?

FROHBIUS: What do you think, my dear Rösel? It is my duty to assist you weak women and put you on guard against perils.

46

RÖSEL: Is it so serious? I only thought Kunze was a little jealous.

FROHBIUS: Jealousy is the work of the Malignant Enemy! I have to try to get him to confession as soon as possible.

RÖSEL: Alas, I feel faint.

FROHBIUS (*approaching*): Don't worry, my dear Rösel. *With cunning:* From now on I will come when Kunze is not at home. Believe me, Kunze is very malignant! Give me a sign every time he goes into the woods to get firewood or when he takes the animals into the city. I will always be ready to give you a word of advice when you are alone.

RÖSEL: It is agreed, dear curate. But what happens if our nosy neighbors notice and tell Kunze?

FROHBIUS (*shrewdly*): Oh, I will go around and jump the fence near the hayloft. Today, are we sure?

RÖSEL: He won't be back until midnight.

FROHBIUS: Then let's be merry and start eating and drinking.

RÖSEL: Eight days ago we killed a fat pig; try my good sausages and drink this wine.

FROHBIUS: Dear and careful woman. Listen! I hear steps.

RÖSEL (*looks outside*): A stranger, he seems to be a beggar.

SCENE 2

Frohbius, Rösel. Enter Kasper.

KASPER: Ah, good evening. My God! What a nice smell of roasted sausage.

FROHBIUS (*mad*): How dare you come in so freely? Get out of here!

RÖSEL: What do you want?

KASPER (*bends down*): Please help me! I am only asking for a mattress for tonight and tomorrow. Then I will go on my way.

FROHBIUS: Go away, rascal!

RÖSEL: Here, take this coin and leave. There is no room here.

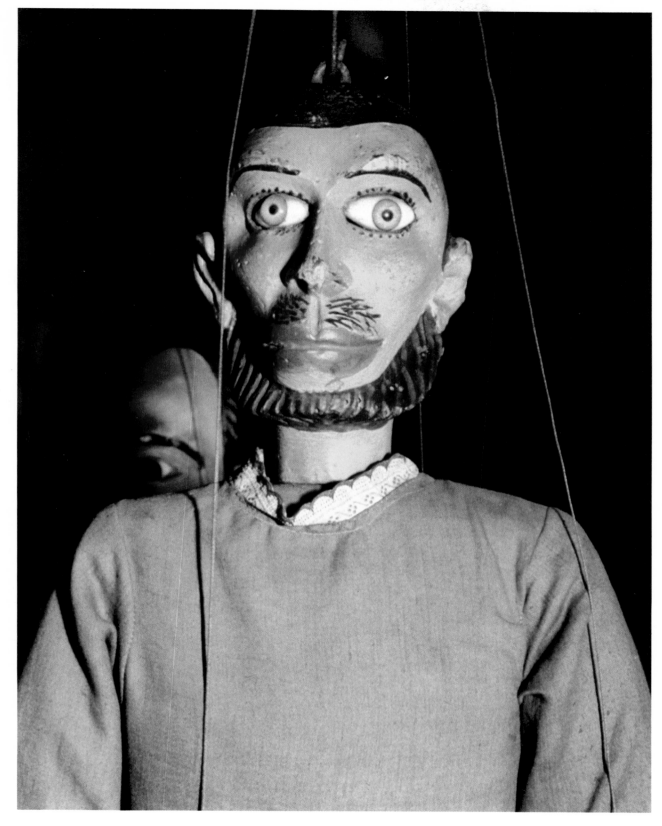

A French marionette from the middle of the nineteenth century with disproportionately large eyes made of glass (ML).

Scene from "The Melting of the Breslavian Bell," presented with characters of the marionette theater of northern Germany in the nineteenth century. The wooden puppets with costumes from the Romantic era were part of the Winter family collection, whose puppeteer tradition dates back to the sixteenth century. Both the characters and the stage were left to the puppet theater of Munich after the death of Adolf Winter, last descendant of the family.

Vagrant professional puppeteers are becoming rare in Western Europe. In East Germany, Rumania, Poland, and Czechoslovakia there are some companies that, with the old characters and scenes, still present the traditional comedies. In Czechoslovakia traditionalists have tried in the last few years to bring back such comedies and to revive Kasparek, related to the German Kasper; but they were unable to compete against the rich ideas and fantasy of Speibl and his son Hurvinek, born during the twenties, and the presentation of marionette films made after the war (PM).

KASPER: I am a poor vagrant artist. I have walked a
lot today. Let me rest until tomorrow. You
won't be sorry.

FROHBIUS: Vagrant artist? Go and hang yourself!

KASPER (*with mockery*): How kind of you! When I am
ordained I would like to be your vicar.

FROHBIUS: There, where the crows come, they'll give
you the tonsure!

KASPER: Don't be so nasty. I am an honest and entertaining type.

FROHBIUS: You are a purse snatcher!

RÖSEL (*to Kasper*): Now leave my house and leave me
in peace. Soon my husband will arrive and he
can't stand strangers.

KASPER (*to himself*): Ah, I understand it. *Aloud:*
Then I'll go, but you will be sorry for your arro-
gance. *To himself:* I will hide someplace, and when
the peasant comes I will play a nasty trick. *He
leaves in a hurry.*

SCENE 3

Frohbius and Rösel.

FROHBIUS: Hurry, close the door so we are not
disturbed.

Rösel goes out and quickly returns.

RÖSEL: I have locked and bolted the door.

FROHBIUS: Now let's eat, drink and be merry.

Someone knocks.

FROHBIUS (*mad*): Who is it now?

RÖSEL: I am going to see. *She goes to the window.* Oh,
my God! It is my husband.

A louder knock.

FROHBIUS (*jumping to his feet*): Saint Quirinus the
martyr! Where can I hide? Where do I go?

RÖSEL: Come on, hurry. Get the wine, the bread, and
the sausage and hide in this room near the oven.
When my husband goes to sleep I will help you
escape.

50

Arlecchino and Pantalone, from a Neopolitan marionette show. The masks are from the commedia dell'arte. *In Italy the marionette theater has always tried to equal the real theater. Since the eighteenth century it has presented operas, and in the nineteenth century in Rome it even presented ballets. The dancers were so similar to real dancers that they had to wear underwear. The Italian puppeteers, due to their innate talent for the puppet theater, became known and admired in Germany, France, and England. Until the twenties the Teatro dei Piccoli of Podrecca with its five hundred puppets and twenty-three animators was considered the most splendid in the world (PM).*

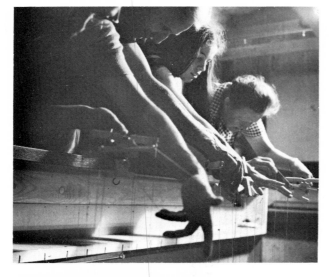

Maneuvering the puppets in difficult movements at the Marionette Theater of Basel. The highest achievement for a marionettist, as for a puppeteer, is success in letting the marionette appear to move on its own.

Frohbius gets the tablecloth with everything on it and runs into the side room. Rösel goes out and returns with Kunze.

SCENE 4

Rösel, Kunze.

KUNZE: My dear Rösel, why have you locked everything up?

RÖSEL: So that the neighbor's pigs won't come into the yard. How come you are so early?

KUNZE: Because we have broken our axes against a hard tree. We had to stop and I had to come back home. I was also getting hungry, so hurry up and roast some sausage. Get me some bread, some bacon, and a pitcher of wine.

RÖSEL: The sausages were eaten a long time ago and there is no wine in the house.

KUNZE: I hear the bells on the cows' necks. Go and see who is in the garden.

RÖSEL: It must be another beggar. I'll chase him away. *She goes to the door, Kasper enters.*

SCENE 5

Rösel, Kunze, and Kasper.

KASPER: Good evening, dear people.

KUNZE: What is it? Who are you?

RÖSEL (*in a low voice only Kasper can hear*): What the devil brings you back?

KASPER (*the same way to Rösel*): If you don't say anything, I won't either.

KUNZE: (*to Kasper*): Speak up—who are you?

KASPER: Listen, I am an apprentice to a great, famous, most knowledgeable and miraculous doctor. We would like to establish ourselves in the nearby village during the feasts. I am preceding him so that I can announce his coming. I am weary from my journey and would like to rest for the night. In exchange I put my knowledge at your disposal.

KUNZE: Well, stay for the night and tell us what it is that you do!

Marionettes used for the grotesque play "Goethe at the Examination" by Alfred Polgar and Egon Friedell, presented for the first time in 1925. They were planned by Olaf Gulbransson for the Marionette and Artists' Theater of Munich, whose director, Paul Brann, through collaboration with writers, theatrical people, painters, architects, and musicians tried to bring to life the idea of an artistic marionette theater (PM).

KASPER: We know how to cure diseases of the eyes and teeth, we can cure calluses on the feet, and we know the ritual to cure a fever. We have potions for every disease and wound. We also practice black magic; we can do spells against fire, predict your future, locate treasures, talk to spirits, and fly through the air as a ghost during the night.

KUNZE: Well! This I'd like to see!

KASPER: I also know how to cure people's whims and make everyone happy. When I go to feasts, weddings, and fairs, everyone becomes serene and my jokes are better than pills and potions.

KUNZE: This is science! You are my man. Come on, wife, bring the supper.

RÖSEL: I only have bread and cheese.

KASPER (to himself): She is a worse lier than I am.

KUNZE (to Kasper): Well, then, we'll have to make do. But first, tell me—years ago I heard that you vagrant artists can also conjure up the Devil; is that so?

KASPER (happy): Yes, by George! It's really nothing. I can conjure up the Devil at any moment. To himself: I am getting an idea! Aloud: Yes, at any moment. Especially during the night, and he has to answer all my questions. And also, if I ask him, he has to bring in roasted sausages, bread, and wine.

KUNZE: It is impossible! There is nothing more that I would like to see than the Devil in person. If you know him, bring him here!

KASPER: Yes, but it is so dangerous. I have to advise you that if anyone speaks only a word, he could destroy us all.

RÖSEL: Oh, no! Leave the Devil out.

KUNZE: Why? We know how to keep quiet. Let him come.

KASPER: Then hold hands and back your way out. Go through the yard to the ladder that goes to the hayloft. Go up the stairs backward, first your wife, then you. But remember: not a single word. In the meantime I will conjure up the Devil with my magic glasses. When I yell "Return," come down

the stairs. Turn yourselves around three times. Hold hands and slowly enter, still backing in. Then you will see the Devil. Remember: not a single word.

KUNZE: Not a word, don't worry. I understand.

KASPER: Now I will clap my hands, and when I count to three, we start. Pay attention. Claps his hands. One! Two! Three!

Kunze and Rösel exit, backing out. Kasper goes toward the door of the side room and lets the priest in.

SCENE 6

Kasper and Frohbius.

KASPER: Now, priest, I have to repay you for your rudeness. I am going to call the peasant and make sure that he gives you one of those beatings you will never forget.

FROHBIUS (trembling): Oh, my dear friend, I beg of you: Help me so I can get out of here.

KASPER (shrewdly): Well! Now I become your friend? Only a short time ago you called me different names.

FROHBIUS: Forgive me, dear man, and help me; if the peasant finds me here he will beat me to death.

KASPER: You deserve it! Why do you run after someone else's wife? If you promise that in the future you will behave, I'll help you.

FROHBIUS: I promise. Here, take these twelve thalers as compensation. I will also give you good lodging, and when we get home I will give you more money.

KASPER (putting the money in his pocket): Come on, priest, do what I tell you: Take off your garments, take some soot from the stove and blacken your hands and your face, then cover yourself with that cowhide I saw in the corner of the little room. When I shout "Come, Devil!" for the third time, come in, roar like a wild bear, and put the wine, the sausages, and the bread that you

54

Scene from "Livietta and Tracallo," comic opera by Giovanni Battista Pergolesi, presented by Ernst Georg Rüegg in 1925 at the Swiss Marionette Theater. "The marionette," says Hans Jelmoli, "this enigmatic creature of the theater, receives from the music its genuine soul. Its movements . . . taken by themselves, are stereotyped and jerky. . . . The musical rhythm corrects the primitive qualities of the puppet and transforms it into an expressive interpreter of every human sentiment (KG)."

The first marionettes of the St. Gall theater, established around 1850. Originally they belonged to Karl Wilhelm von Heideck, an artistic lieutenant-general from Bavaria. With them, Franz Pocci, master of ceremonies and music director for King Louis I of Bavaria, performed before the Bavarian nobility. The puppets and the little theater, complete with every imaginable kind of mechanism, were given by Count Pocci to the puppeteer Josef Schmid, who added them to his own, to complete his theater in Munich. Around 1900 they were acquired by Hermann Scherrer-Gehrig, a merchant of St. Gall, who in 1903 formed the first permanent Swiss marionette theater (PP, Historic Museum of St. Gall).

took with you down here. The rest will happen by itself and you can leave peacefully. Now hurry, go into the room.

The priest goes.

SCENE 7

Kasper alone.

KASPER (*calls through the door*): Return!
Kunze and Rösel return, walking backward into the room.

Now stand here. Do not move and do not talk if you care to live. I have already conjured up the Devil and I locked him in that room. Wait! Here I have a piece of chalk. You never know! It is better not to take chances. I will make a magic circle so that the Devil cannot harm us. *He draws a circle around Kunze and Rösel, also putting himself inside it with them, and then calls aloud:*

> I call you for the first time.
> Come out from your infernal refuge,
> Put in the circle a bottle of wine,
> Also sausages, cake, and bread.
> For the second time I call you.
> Come here to me, in front of this circle.
> For the third time I beg of you,
> Obey and listen to me!
> Devil, come!

The priest enters dressed as the Devil, blackened, with the cowhide on his shoulders. Roaring, he puts down the wine and food in the circle.

KASPER: Devil, go round the circle and let us watch you.

The Devil roars and goes around the circle three times. Kunze trembles and wants to talk. Kasper closes his mouth with his hand.

KASPER: Devil, now stop. Now you can leave this house by the door, the chimney, or the fireplace, but make sure you do not destroy anything. Do you understand, Devil? Now go!

The Devil roars and runs out of the door.

58

SCENE 8

All of the above except Frohbius.

KASPER (*goes out of the circle*): Now you can talk. Luckily the Devil has left.

KUNZE: Alas! I perspire from fear. Hurry, erase the circle so the Devil will not return.

KASPER (*erases the circle with his foot*): Now, tell me why you wanted to see the Devil.

KUNZE: I never imagined he was so black, hairy, deformed, and horrible. I believe I would have gone crazy if I had been alone. And that frightening roar, those eyes of fire, those horns, and those terrible fangs protruding from his mouth. To tell the truth, I fear that the Devil will visit me in my dreams.

KASPER (*laughs*): He is not that terrible. Ha, ha, ha, ha! The Devil was happy that I let him go. He had more fear of you than you of him.

KUNZE: What? The Devil fears me?

RÖSEL (*to Kunze*): Leave the Devil alone and go to sleep. The Devil is back to Hell by now.

KASPER (*drinks*): Then you don't want to taste his wine?

KUNZE: No, now I will go to bed, wearing a blessed chain around my neck. You can remain in this room. Rösel will prepare your bed. For compensation I give you a florin. Now, good night! *He goes out.*

SCENE 9

Rösel and Kasper.

RÖSEL: For the rest of my life I will never forget this night. I feared you would talk. My husband would have killed him, since he hates him.

KASPER: He has good reason, so get it into your head: Be a good wife and resist the priest with firmness.

RÖSEL: You are right. Now you can make yourself comfortable here. Tomorrow I will give you five florins and will prepare a good breakfast for you. *She goes out.*

Bastienne from "Bastien and Bastienne" by W. A. Mozart.
This musical comedy was produced in 1923 by Paul
Bodmer for the Swiss Marionette Theater of Zurich. The
figures were, like most others of that theater, the work of
Carl Fischer, who was a teacher of woodworking at the
School of Arts and Trades in Zurich. Puppets that were
once made by the puppeteer himself were created by a
specialist working on projects of painters and sculptors
(KG).

The French Polichinelle.

Chanchet (Ciancès) and Naness of Liège and Tournai.

Lafleur of Picardy.

SCENE 10

Kasper alone.

KASPER: By George! I am content with this celebration. With this story of the Devil and the priest I will make good money. Now I have to think of my stomach; this situation has given me a good appetite, and the roasted sausages will do just fine. *He sits at the table.*

> While the peasant dreams of the Devil,
> So that it won't get sour,
> I will drink the wine.

Hurray. *He drinks.*

The curtain falls.

The word *marionette* is derived from the French. It was used for the first time in 1600 in a work by Guillaume Bouchet. Its origin has not been definitely determined. According to Charles Magnin (a puppet scholar), the word was derived from

"Hansjoggel" was a character from Zurich. It was used
in 1923 by R. J. Welti as a local figure, in place of
Kasper. It had been carved by Carl Fischer. Welti made
it talk in the plain dialect of Zurich. Hansjoggel had an
enormous success as the servant who created a great deal
of confusion in "Faust" (KG).

Marionette theater at the end of the eighteenth century. From a vignette in an almanac of the time.

by strings. The puppeteer moves the real marionette from above with the help of a guide cross to which all the strings are attached. He pulls up, turns, or lowers the cross, activating, at the same time, a more or less complex system of levers and stops which are attached to the cross. With such an apparatus, the hand of a master can really obtain marvelous mimic effects. The puppet made of wood, cloth, rope, papier-mâché, and today even of plastic can perform a great number of sequential, coordinated movements in a homogeneous fashion. These movements can characterize any aspect of reality or fantasy in such a convincing way that a well-guided puppet can compete with real actors and even surpass them.

Actually, the sole ambition of the marionette theater up to the present century was to imitate the live theater. And after Hanswurst was expelled from the stage during the period of Gottsched (beginning of the eighteenth century) the marionette theater followed the tradition of the popular Baroque theater with its repertoire of chivalrous dramas, melodramas, and ghost stories.[26]

The charm of the puppet theater and its extraordinary interpretive possibilities exercised a great attraction on the artists of the nineteenth century. In 1773–75 Goethe wrote his *Urfaust* under the influence of a puppet show about Dr. Faust he had seen in his youth. (There is documentary evidence that the presentation of the puppet play "Faust" had taken place in Tübingen as early as 1588.) Even by the eighteenth century, the educational values of puppets had been discovered. Goethe as a boy had received a little marionette theater as a gift from his father, and the German Romantic writers Achim von Arnim and Clemens Brentano had learned about puppet and shadow shows as children in Frankfurt.

The Romantic poets, who eagerly gathered the treasures of popular literature, were enthusiastic about the secular puppet theater. For them it was not merely a popular heritage worth being saved but an inspirational reference for their works. Among

Marion, a character of a pastoral show of the thirteenth century, or from the moving figures of the Maries of the medieval nativity scenes, or from *marotte*, the clown's cane. J. B. Frisch, in his German-Latin dictionary of 1741, relates it to the medieval clown Mario, or Morione.

Marionette, in French, is used to signify any theatrical grouping. In the international terminology of the puppet show this term is used exclusively for a flexible puppet attached to a steel bar or hung

62

The drummer, created for a show based on Claude Debussy's La Boîte à joujoux, *was created in 1918 by Otto Morach for the Swiss Marionette Theater. Morach, teacher of painting at the School of Arts and Trades of Zurich, contributed his very expressive marionettes to "Faust" (C. W. Wiegand, Jakob Welti), "The Puppet Show of Master Pedro" (Manuel de Falla), "Kasane" (Walter Lesch), and others. His contribution helped the success of the Swiss Marionette Theater and the similar organization of Zurich (KG).*

those who were inspired by the puppet theater are: Arnim, Andreas Kerner, Christian Grabbe, Nikolaus Lenau, and Eduard Mörike. Joseph von Eichendorff, in his puppet show "The Unknown," developed a political and social satire on the times which simultaneously had a fable-like marionette unreality about it. August Iffland, with his comedy "The Marionette" (1807), and August von Kotzebue, in his "Count of Gleichen," a "living marionette show" (also 1807), struck with irony and mockery at the Romantic passion for the marionette. During the Romantic period the poet Theodor Storm wrote what could well be the best story in the wide and enchanting field of the literature on puppets and puppeteers, *Pole Puppenspieler* (1874).

The possibility of using marionettes in a conventional theater (see the critical essay of Heinrich von Kleist, "About the Marionette Theater") corresponded to the artistic sensibility of the Romantics. More than once, it came to mind that the puppet theater could be substituted for the live theater. In the words of Ludwig Tieck, "educate the people through the marionette."

In the dialogue between "Bruno," a gentleman who eats his morning breakfast with satisfaction, and "Grigio," a director of the Popular Theater, who at first is eaten up by unexpressed rage and then gradually starts to complain in a loud voice, the writer E. T. A. Hoffmann, in 1818, made some comparisons between marionettes and actors.[27] Bruno is presented as the owner of a vagrant theater—without worries, with no problem of replacing the old actors or those who leave, and with no preoccupations concerning manuscripts or staging.

BRUNO: Ah! Everything I say about the comedies and the actors I choose you are free to assume is a lie, but it is as I say. After many bitter experiences, I was finally able to form a company which, for its excellence, and above all for its unbelievable harmony, has not yet given me any disappointment, only happiness. There is not even a member of the company, who, concerning direction, costuming,

64

Marionettes for Carl Maria von Weber's opera "Abu Hassan," as staged by Pierre Gauchat in 1942 for the Zurich Marionettes. The puppets were carved by Carl Fischer. With this work and with Pergolesi's "The Maestro of Music," already staged by Gauchat in 1930, a group of puppet-show lovers revived the Swiss Marionette Theater, which had become extinct in 1935, as the Zurich

Marionettes. A prominent place was given to musical comedy and to opera, with works by Gluck, Pergolesi, Offenbach, Donizetti, Mozart, and Hindemith being staged. But fables and comedies written or elaborated on exclusively for the puppet theater, by Hauff, Grimm, Gozzi, Edwin Arnet, Richard Seewald, Peter and Jakob Welti, Traugott Vogel, and Herbert Meier, were also presented. The staging was provided by those artists who had already collaborated with the Swiss Marionette Theater, such as Otto Morach, Ernst Gubler, Pierre Gauchat, Max Tobler, and Eugen Früh. New contributors were Sita Jucker, Eduard Gunziger, Richard Seewald, Jörg Zimmermann, J. Muller-Brockmann, and Hans Städeli (ST).

and everything else, doesn't blindly yield to my will and interpret his part just as asked, even to the smallest detail.

GRIGIO: No rebels? Never any opposition?

BRUNO: Never! Besides, everyone learns his or her part to perfection without ever daring a change or omission. We always act without a prompter.

GRIGIO: It isn't possible! Even when the actors memorize their parts, as soon as they don't see that head in the prompter's box they get discouraged.

BRUNO: We act without a prompter, and yet there is never an obstacle, never an instant of fright or hesitation. May I add that, in entering a scene or leaving one, or in forming a group on stage, there is no confusion, since no one dares get ahead at the expense of others. You can imagine the pleasant harmony of our shows. This is also the result of the mutual understanding and fondness they have for each other. Up to now, never a fight. It is unbelievable that my artists make very few requests and are satisfied with their low salary.

GRIGIO: Artists! Actors! Few requests? Low salary! You are making fun of me! Where did you find these types of people?

BRUNO: They are at my disposal constantly, since I find young talent desiring to dedicate itself to the art everywhere. Just the other day I engaged a young man with a magnificent physique, incomparable talent, and a noble heart.

GRIGIO: What are you saying, sir? I hope you have no intention of recruiting actors from my theater? Keep in mind that each of them is used to better things and none of them would be willing to be part of a vagrant company.

BRUNO: But what are you thinking? None of your actors could be of any use to me.

GRIGIO: Then I have to change my opinion of your theater's excellence, since you don't find my good artists useful.

BRUNO: That's not it exactly. It is my principle to employ only those artists who have never put a foot in the theater.

GRIGIO: And these inexperienced young people . . .

66

BRUNO: After only a few hours of my instruction, they act in such a perfect way that it is impossible to distinguish them from actors of much more experience.

GRIGIO: Ah! Now I understand! Just as before with your dramatic dream, now you tease me with your ideal type of company . . . the way the actors should be! It is just a chimera born from your ironic and jovial fantasy.

BRUNO: Not at all. My company has followed me to this hotel. Its members are in the rooms above our heads.

GRIGIO: What? They are here and I don't hear any noise? I don't hear any one talking or humming. No one laughs, no one goes up and down the stairs, nor calls the waiter? No one prepares the breakfast, either hot or cold? No one tinkles the glasses? Is it possible?

BRUNO: Yes! This quiet behavior is one of the primary virtues of my company. I bet that they all have gathered in one room to memorize their parts.

Grigio cannot comprehend such an ideal arrangement and begs Bruno to lead him to see this remarkable ensemble. It turns out to be "a large number of marionettes, some of which are the most beautiful and well proportioned he has ever seen!"

Only Count Franz Pocci elevated the vagrant theater of marionettes from a show for fairs to the level of the artistic theater. In 1858, in Munich, he had helped the archivist Josef Leonhard Schmid, later called Papa Schmid, to establish a marionette theater. Count Pocci remained a faithful and steady patron of the theater he had established throughout his life. Pocci wrote approximately fifty puppet comedies during the end of the Romantic period. Even today their delightful combination of fable and irony still belongs to the classic repertoire of the marionettes' theater.[28]

The marionette theater founded by Papa Schmid had wide influence. It induced Anton Aicher to create the Salzburger Marionetten and inspired

Rod "cabaret" character, about sixty inches high, from the original Zurich puppet theater of Fred Schneckenburger. Schneckenburger gave great importance to the abstract puppet to convey the theatrical message. He used to say, "The nature and the task of the puppet theater is to do and say things that the real theater cannot do or say."

other puppet theaters in Germany, Austria, and
Switzerland.

Following an extended stay in Munich, Hermann
Scherrer-Gehrig, merchant and future town coun-
cilman, established in 1903 the first permanent
Swiss marionette theater from the regulars of the
marionette theater of Papa Schmid. The puppets
were those originally belonging to Count Pocci, who,
in the role of master of ceremonies to the king of
Bavaria, had performed at times in front of the court.
The St. Gall Marionette Theater founded by
Scherrer-Gehrig existed until 1943 and served as a
model for almost all the Swiss marionette theaters,
even though they followed new methods of show
format and conception. A great number of artists
and puppeteers of the twentieth century did not regard the puppet theater as merely a copy of real

theater. They renounced a naturalistic concept, suc-
ceeding in increasing the expressive strength, gro-
tesqueness, and vivacity of the puppets. The impetus
for the major evolution of the contemporary Swiss
marionette theater came in 1914 as a result of an
exhibition on modern theater held in the School of
Arts and Trades in Zurich. The exhibition was organized by Gordon Craig and Adolphe Appia, pioneers of the modern theater. The school's director,
Alfred Altherr, commented:

In relation to his own scenes, radically opposed to
all naturalistic motives, Gordon Craig presented
an exhibition of magnificent theater masks, and
marionettes from Java and Burma which aroused
some justified interest. Another exhibition that
gave a lasting impression was the presentation of

By the eighteenth century, operas were being presented by marionettes. The Swiss Marionette Theater made ample use of opera and musical comedy. "Bethly" by Hans Jelmoli, taken from an opera of Gaetano Donizetti and elaborated for the marionette theater, was a big hit. The puppets, such as the two soldiers shown in this illustration from the opera première in 1925, were designed by the painter Ernst Gubler (KG).

marionettes given at the same time by Munich's artists in the Museum of Arts and Trade. These shows promoted the idea of creating a similar theater in Switzerland. New artistic directions of a totally different nature were established in the programs. The "great" theater, due to its dependence on actors, set designers, and special-effects creators, was not suited to innovation in the Appia or Craig style. For this reason the smaller puppet theaters with their obedient wooden puppets lent themselves to the introduction and diffusion of new ideas. In presenting the old puppet shows it was important to avoid the pure and simple imitation of the "great" theater. All accessories of secondary importance had to be removed from the scene. Such items as furniture and materials which were too naturalistic were taken out in order not to give the impression of a dollhouse. The marionette also had to be given a simple environment to avoid the almost photographic imitation of life. As time went by it reached an abstraction that can well be considered the true style of the marionette.[29]

In 1918, in collaboration with the puppet show given on the occasion of the first large exhibition of the *Schweizerischer Werkbund,* the School of Arts and Trades of Zurich and its collaborators were successful in establishing a permanent marionette theater. The beginning was not easy, since they had to assure the collaboration of the local writers in order to obtain theatrical works suited to the taste of the times, and to acquire ·the necessary experience in set design and technical direction. From the beginning, the new possibility of the musical comedy presented as an opera for marionettes was foreseen.

The early avant-garde efforts of these presentations were reenforced by contact with the Dada movement, founded in Zurich in 1916. The assistance of the Dadaists was a great advantage to the new institution. Even more fortunate, perhaps, was the fact that artistic contributions were made by famous painters, sculptors, and musicians, and many artisans. Among the participants were: Henri Bischoff, Sophie Taeuber-Arp, Paul Bodmer, Ernst Gubler, Karl Hügin, Louis Moilliet, Otto Morach, E. Isler, E. G. Rüegg, Max Tobler, and Rudolf Urech, who helped in designing scenes and other projects. Carl Fischer designed and sculpted puppets, sometimes using models by others. The musicians Gustave Doré, Hans Jelmoli, H. Dubs, Paul Müller, A. Schaichet, E. Krenek, Manuel de Falla, and J. J. Nater gave their valuable contributions, as did many Swiss writers and men of letters like René Morax, Traugott Vogel, Jakob Welti, and Werner Wolf, in addition to a series of narrators and singers. They all cooperated to bring the new marionette theater from the amateur level to that of an artistic institution. The most passionate promoter of all was Alfred Altherr.

The example of the Zurich marionette theater was soon followed by similar organizations in the rest of Switzerland. The first of such attempts was in Lausanne by the Arch. Mercier in collaboration with Baud-Bovy, René Morax, Henri Bischoff, and Alexandre Cingria. This was followed, in 1926, by the theater in the Bernese Oberland initiated by Fritz Ringgenberg and the painter Arnold Brügger. In Bienne one could have attended the artistic marionette shows of Fernand and Elsi Giauque. Among the approximately two dozen puppet companies that are still active in Switzerland today, there exist three major marionette theaters that own their own buildings and have regular shows. The shows given by two famous foreign marionette theaters, in the period between the two wars, stimulated the still-active directors of Basel and Geneva to organize local groups. They were the Teatro dei Piccoli of Podrecca, which more than forty years earlier had enchanted Marcelle Moynier in Geneva, and the Munich Marionette and Artists' Theater, directed by Paul Brann, who influenced Richard Koelner in Basel. In 1956, the St. Gall Puppet Theater was organized.

Up to the beginning of the sixties three other important theater groups maintained their activi-

The snake from "The Show of the Original Sin" by
Jakob Flach, presented for the first time by the Marionette
Theater of Ascona. Flach was rapidly able to interest
important musicians, sculptors, painters, and writers in
his theater. Over the course of nearly fifteen years—the
theater was born in 1960—forty-seven of the sixty-two
works presented were created by members of the Asconese
group (ST).

ties. They were: the one owned by Erich Weiss in Winterthur and Zurich, whose monumental style detached itself from the norm; the one owned by Jakob Flach, who during World War II succeeded in Ascona in getting many authors, musicians, sculptors, and scene painters to contribute to his marionette theater; and the "Zurich Marionettes," which disbanded at the same time as the Ascona group, after having followed the tradition of the Swiss Marionette Theater for the twenty years after World War II. It had been this group and the puppet "cabaret" of Fred Schneckenburger that had attracted to Zurich the attention of the international specialists in that field.

The promotion of puppet shows was strengthened during the last decade by the Union Internationale de la Marionnette (UNIMA), which has in turn been remarkably influenced by developments in the West, where the puppet show is recognized as a means for children's education and therapeutic teaching. In Switzerland the innovations of Therese Keller have been especially noteworthy. Throughout Europe she has urged many parents and educators to assemble and present their own puppet shows. Another professional of equal talent is Käthy Wüthrich. And for more than a decade Peter W. Loosli, a professional in the field, has been famous for his marionette shows. The Rumanian marionettist Pierre Pedroff has recently found a new way of presenting his shows by using *marottes à main* (rod puppets with a human hand that works simultaneously),

and his countryman Michel Poletti, who lives in Ticino, is also an innovator. In addition to those theaters already established, some recently founded groups are trying to overcome preconceived notions about puppet shows. Besides marionettes and puppets, they are making increasing use of rod and shadow figures. Werner Flück works with such figures in the children's hour on Swiss-German television. The puppet theaters of Switzerland have formed an organization that regularly publishes a magazine, *Puppenspiel und Puppenspieler*. Anyone interested in this fascinating means of expression can become a member, because the organization's aim is to introduce this field of work, through courses and seminars, to school and kindergarten teachers, mothers, and educators. (Headquarters are at Michelstrasse 40, Zurich 8049.) [30]

The development of the modern puppet theater would not have been possible without the influence of the puppet theater outside Europe, particularly the rich and fantastic world of Asiatic shadow figures, rod marionettes, and puppets. The rod puppet, which combines the vitality of the true puppet and the charm of the marionette, has exerted a special fascination upon artists and puppeteers. One need only remember the pretty Java figures of the *wajang golek* theater to understand this. The most beautiful European creations of this type of puppet are those of Richard Teschner in Vienna. Aspects of the Oriental puppet theater are dealt with in the following chapters.

Japanese *Bunraku* Theater

The origin of the classical Japanese puppet theater dates back to the *Kugutsu-sci*. They were hunters who during their periods of rest performed puppet shows, going from door to door. Later they propagated the ideas of the Jodo Buddhist sect and presented scenes from Buddha's life with their puppets. The popularity of such traveling shows was increased by the fact that in these shows *sekkyo* (sermons of lay Buddhists) were sung.

In Niscinomya these puppet shows were given by some geishas who, to entertain their clients, accompanied the presentation with songs. The sacred aspect of the *kugutsu* (so-called in honor of the old hunters) was totally lost. Not until the end of the sixteenth century did the ancient form of the puppet show develop into the popular style still in existence in the *bunraku*. Bunraku-ken was the stage name of a puppeteer from the island of Awaci, where the rural theater had formerly been cultivated. In 1845 he founded a permanent theater for his puppets in the affluent city of Osaka. It was named after him and became known as Bunraken-za (*Bun* = literature, *raku* = pleasure, *za* = house). Since then, *bunraku* has come to mean a puppet show in a permanent theater with a permanent stage.

The Bunraku Theater of Osaka, the only one still in existence, is the exact replica of the original. Bunraken-za burned down in 1926. The stage is similar to a bridge about twenty inches high, which occupies almost entirely the rear portion of the rectangular theater. The puppets act on the higher level, maneuvered by puppeteers from the lower one. If the puppeteer wants to become a little taller he wears buskin-like sandals about five inches high. To his right and at the same height as the stage, there is a revolving platform.

Scarcely has the clapping of some wooden sticks announced the beginning of the presentation than there is a movement of the platform and the *gidayu* (singer-narrator) and his accompanist, who plays the *samisen,* appear, dressed in ceremonial costumes. A stage manager, dressed in a cloak and black hat, introduces them to the public. The *samisen* player performs fast and exciting tunes on his lute-like instrument. Then he comes back into harmony with the narration and the singer intervenes. The puppet enters the scene, cautious, full of nobility, detached and odd, moved rhythmically by his guide in synchronization with the *samisen.* He performs well within our view, held up by puppeteers dressed in black, in precise accord with the singer-narrator. The *gidayu,* who sits at the right of the *samisen* player, has the text before him on a polished and decorated reading desk. His pathetic narration has an increasing intensity, augmented with gestures. He always speaks in a rhythm of his own, changing the tempo at his pleasure.

Making violent faces, expressing sorrow, the singer-narrator raises his voice as the drama requires. He cries along with the puppet, expressing the range of human feelings with incredible variety. Soon one gets the impression that these . . . emotions can almost enter the inanimate figure on the stage and that the human words come from the puppet's lips. It appears to talk and act humanly, in a mysterious and devilish manner. . . .

In our imagination, the puppet starts, little by little, to free himself from his guides, making them appear to be unimportant shadows. At most, they become a magic background in front of which he rises as though having a will of his own in his small moving head. The puppet is only under the control of the metronome, which measures the tempo of the *samisen* player. In no

73

1

2

3

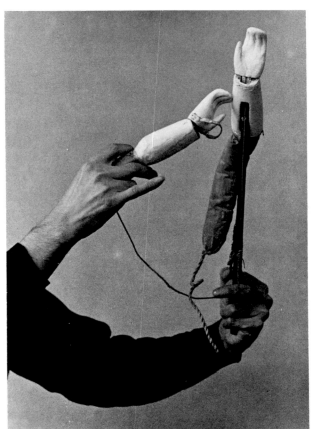

4

1 *Rendezvous on the palace balcony. The puppets act on a different level from that of their animators, whose black clothes against the vivid colors of the scenes and costumes appear almost invisible.*

2 *The animators, covered with black cloaks and hoods, before entering the scene. At the right is the master puppeteer wearing buskin-style sandals.*

3 *This head—as the black-painted lips tell—belongs to a refined lady. The lips and the eyelashes are moved by little levers at the base of the neck.*

4 *Two animators share the movements of the arms. The scissors-like system in the left arm serves to guide the arm from a certain distance; the iron piece curved above the right wrist serves to hold a sword.*

75

Bunraku *puppet. In Japan there are several kinds of puppet theater: The* noroma ningyo, *with puppets on rods, is the oldest, while the* bunraku *is the most artistic. The Japanese also are familiar with shadow shows, true puppets, marionettes, and the* kuruma ningyo, *a simplified version of the* bunraku *with only one animator to each puppet.*

The bunraku *puppet is guided by three animators. One moves the feet, another the left arm, and the master puppeteer the head and the right arm. The classic* bunraku *theater had about forty puppeteers, twenty-five to thirty narrators, and as many* samisen *players, in addition to the stagehands (PM).*

other way does he allow himself to be flattered, lured, cajoled, or in any other way distracted from his intention to interpret his part to the end, to serve the magic law of his stage life to which he is destined by the enigmatic artistic will of man.[31]

The *bunraku* puppet is half to three quarters the size of a man. It is guided by two, or at the most three, movements (*nunghyozukai*) that are in complete accord with the *jōruri*. The *jōruri* is the dialogue, which is partly sung and partly narrated by the *gidayu* in a lyric-epic style.

Since the *bunraku* theaters with their *jōruri* were so successful, many of the famous dramatists came to write texts for puppets. Even the major Japanese dramatist Chikamatsu Monzaemon (1653–1725), was an excellent *jōruri* singer and theater man. He collaborated with Takemoto Gidayu, the singer-narrator who has given his name to all the singer-narrators following him.

The major competitor of the *bunraku* theater was the popular actors' theater, *kabuki,* which has existed since the 1600's alongside the puppet theater, forcing the latter to search for ever more striking effects. "The puppet learned to move his fingers, to open his mouth, to close his eyes, to move his eyebrows. One man alone cannot control the precious toy. Two helpers assist him: One, seated, moves the puppet's feet; the other, to his left—with the help of a scissors-like system—moves the left arm. The master puppeteer controls the right hand and the head, the full weight of the puppet, and its expressions. He has to coordinate its movements skillfully so that all its limbs will move in harmony." [32] The puppeteers are covered with a black cloak and hood. The black, against the intense colors of the scenery and costumes, becomes almost invisible. Only the master puppeteer is at times permitted to appear in silk clothes or in old ceremonial costumes (*kamiscimo*).

After the middle of the eighteenth century, the technique and the repertoire of the *bunraku* theater became so refined and reached such perfection that it surpassed the competitive *kabuki* theater. To regain the public interest, the *kabuki* theater undertook dramatic puppet presentations and recitations. These puppets became teachers to the actors of *kabuki*. Even the *jōruri* were imitated on the *kabuki* stage. This healthy competition brought both theaters to their supreme perfection.

78

Shadow Shows

Introduction

When the sultan Saladin asked al-Qâdi al-Fâdil if he had liked the show, he answered: "I witnessed a great lesson. I saw some rich people come and go, and when the curtain dropped there was only one person who moved them." [33]

Wu-ti, emperor of China, of the Han dynasty, was suffering; his favorite wife, Wang, had died. No one could comfort him. The arts and the jokes of the comedian and the clown were too vulgar for him; the tales of the narrators were too boring; the rare foods too tasteless; and not even his many concubines succeeded in comforting him. But the god of kindness was with him. Sciao-wong (also called Ciao-meng) arrived at the court of the em-

Silhouettes: a popular art form still cultivated in China.

peror and offered to make the ghost of the beautiful Wang appear. Thus, the emperor Wu-ti sat night after night before a stretched screen in front of a door, behind which the spirit of his favorite wife appeared. They would talk about the marvelous days and nights that they had spent together; they reviewed affairs of state and gossiped about the daily intrigues of the court. One day the emperor's love for Wang was so strong that, breaking his own promise not to touch the screen or look behind it, he tore it apart and saw Sciao-wong holding a cutout figure with whose shadows he had evoked the illusion of the spirit of Wang. According to some, the emperor, angered at having been deceived, had Sciao-wong tortured and decapitated, as well as the court dignitaries he thought involved in this effort to control the affairs of state. According to others, Sciao-wong was granted the title of Marshal and given a fortune, in exchange for his promise to continue making the image of Wang appear and to instruct others in this art.

All this occurred, supposedly, in the year 120 B.C. But according to the *T'an-su* (*T'u-sciu-tsi-ci'ung*), the huge 5,000-volume Chinese encyclopedia of the eleventh century, the shadow show must have originated during the Sung dynasty, at the time of the reign of Jöng-tsung (1023–1065). "Traveling narrators added shadow figures to the popular presentation of the 'History of Three Kingdoms' (San-kuo)." We can imagine this to be something similar to the narrations of ballad singers which were once performed at the annual fairs. In spite of this, the Wu-ti legends deserve our interest. They show that the Chinese want to establish their priority even in the field of the shadow theater: "China is the birthplace of the shadow show in all its forms found throughout the world." [34] However, researchers have a somewhat different opinion. The oldest docu-

Drawings by Count Franz Pocci for his poems about shadow figures, "The Fat Gentleman" and "The Serenade."

ments on the shadow show can be found in India. There, in the Sitabenga Cave (state of Sarguja), the controversial proof of a shadow theater dating back to the second century B.C. has been discovered. Many scholars see in the semi-epic *Mahabharata*, composed by Hanuman, the oldest shadow show. Hanuman appears in the *Ramayana*, an old epic poem containing 24,000 verses which describe the life of Rama, son of King Dasciadha of Ajodhya and supposedly written by Walmiki in the fourth or third century B.C. Even the *Mahanataka* speaks of the battles and adventures of Rama and his lovely and faithful wife Sita.[35] The legends of the *Ramayana* and *Mahabharata* are found also in the shadow shows of Indonesia (Java, Bali), as in those of Thailand, Cambodia, and Malaysia.

On the other hand, coming back to the Wu-Ti legend, the story corresponds in every way to what the shadow show meant at its religious origins: an evocation of the dead. The shadows were originally spirits recalled by evocators, or remembrances of the dead. These spirits were represented by figures artistically cut out from paper or leather and seen in profile on the screen.[36] For this reason, the screen, the stretched cloth that separates the viewer from the figure and from those who make it move, is called in China "Screen of Death." In Java it is called "Fog and Clouds"; in Turkey, "Curtain of the Departing" (of the hour of death); in Arabia, "Screen of Dreams, Veil of the Omnipotent Secret." With the shadow show, we find ourselves in the area where shadows, dreams, and death meet. In many countries the shadow is equated with death, and this kind of show is, as no other, a secret spell, magic.

The elements of the shadow show are:

The screen: a simple sheet stretched on an adjustable frame in the traveling Indian puppet shows; silk in the court shows; nettle fabric or paper for the Chinese poor; a fine cotton cloth in Java; parchment in North Africa and Egypt; ground glass in the modern presentations of England and America.

The light: a lit torch or fagot; candles; sunlight

Dancer of Tolu Bommalata, an Indian shadow show. The oldest and most famous Indian figures for the shadow theater date back to the latter part of the nineteenth century and come from southern India. Their height varies from forty to forty-eight inches. They are made from sheep or goat skin, are painted in colors, and are transparent. The figures are fitted on a rod which is broken into two parts for holding them. If the arms are movable, small rods are attached at the hands. The performances are given in the open, on streets and in plazas; often the screen is only a sari stretched on a transportable frame of the traveling comedians. The light comes from oil lamps, and on the screen appear the stories of gods and heroes such as those told in the old Ramayana and Mahabharata (VB).

coming into a dark room through a window covered with cloth; oil, kerosene or electric light.

The figures: made of dark material (such as cardboard, leather, wood, metal) in the true shadow show, to which belong also the shows made with the movements of the hands (manual shadow show) or with human figures (human shadow show); made of paper, parchment, very thin leather soaked in oil, plastic, or any other similar materials which are transparent, colored or painted, in the so-called colored shadow show; such figures are found in the West, in the Turkish show of Karagöz, in India, and in China. A peculiarity of the Javanese *wajang kulit* figures is that they appear as shadows to the women, who are seated in front of the screen, whereas the men, who are behind the screen, can see the actual figures, beautifully painted.

We already mentioned the diffusion of the shadow show from India to Cambodia, Thailand, Malaysia, and Java. The Chinese shadow show arrived at the time of the Mongol migration into Persia and elsewhere in the Near East. From there it was propagated by the traveling theater, by the gypsies, and by the begging Islamic Monks known as "dervishes."

"Cambaspina" and "the professor," abstract shadow figures by the Dutchman Pieter van Gelder (about 1920).

Ancient Egyptian figure for the shadow show, made of perforated camel leather. The openings are covered with very thin colored skins.

82

Les Ombres chinoises.
He! l'Ami!___quelle heure
est-il?

Etching by Chodowiecki representing a shadow show in Berlin around 1790. The great success of the shadow theater between 1760 and 1830 was paralleled by a vogue for figures in its style, which at that period was at its peak. They were carried as ornaments, hung on walls, and the "Chinese shadows," as they were called, were painted on utensils and china sets. It was enchanting to see them moving at the theater accompanied by words and songs.

It is known that during the eleventh century shadow shows were given in the courts and in the castles of the Seljuks. From the thirteenth century texts of Arab shadow shows come to us, and between the twelfth and seventeenth centuries Egypt was a center of the shadow show in the Islam area.[37]

The route of the shadow show from Egypt to the East is linked to a gloomy and cruel legend: In 1517 the Ottoman Turkish sultan Selim I, conquering Egypt, captured also the last Mameluke sultan, Tūmān Bey, and immediately hanged him. Later he asked a master of shadow shows to present this scene. He was so enthusiastic over the presentation that he invited him to Istanbul to show it to his son Soliman, who later besieged Vienna. From Istanbul the shadow show was brought to Italy, and then, in the seventeenth century, by traveling Italian gypsies and comedians, it was brought into Germany, then France, and ultimately England.

A devil from the book by Lemercier de Neuvilles, Les Pupazzi Noirs (c. 1890), in which the then well known puppeteer made the technique of the shadow show familiar to a larger public.

83

Shadow figures by Séraphin, Paris, 1812.

We could give valid arguments to place the birth of the shadow show in North Africa (Tunis), where the figures are of a single color, black. The supposition exists also that shadow shows were brought to Europe by Europeans traveling in Asia. This explains the fact that they were known as "Chinese shadows." (They were usually connected with a marionette show in some European countries.) This name could also have been derived from the passion of the Rococo period for everything Chinese. In any

case, at that time the shadow show had great success all over Europe. In France at the end of the eighteenth century it was introduced in court through the Spectacle des Énfants de France of Dominique Séraphin, established in Versailles and later moved to the Palais Royal in Paris. In Germany, because of its dream atmosphere, it greatly influenced the Romantic movement and found passionate followers and promoters among painters and poets. It was at times as popular as the puppet and marionette

84

Richly dressed Szechwan figure in the Chinese shadow show. The proportions and movements of the Chinese shadow figures are so perfectly arranged that "every movement has its own center of gravity," as Heinrich von Kleist said also of the marionette. "It is necessary only to hold this center, inside the figure, and the limbs will follow docilely, mechanically by themselves" (VB).

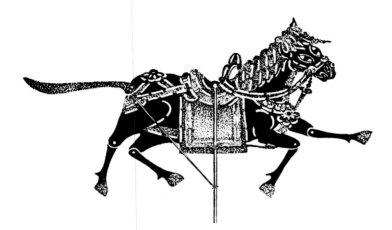

Horse with saddle. The tail is moved by the rod guide, the legs hang loosely.

theater, but it never quite reached their lasting popularity.

A way to propagate this art further was introduced just after World War I by Lotte Reiniger, among others, who used the shadow show for cinematographic purposes: In his fable films this art fully developed its technical and artistic possibilities. Only in Asia is the shadow show still cultivated according to its old traditions, as a heritage deeply rooted in the national culture, as in China, Indonesia, and India. In these countries it is now promoted by governments as an educational tool to fight illiteracy, and while it is proving successful in this effort, it is at the same time losing its importance as a mediator between the gods and men.

China

How can one not love the young ladies of Szechwan? When they go to the temple, it is impossible for them to refuse to go to the temple's feast, where comedians and jugglers perform, where artisans and merchants display their merchandise, while young men court the young ladies. They go elegantly dressed and full of pride—these are two of

86

their principal virtues. Even while being abducted by some terrible bandit, or when they see their lover possessed by the Devil, or when they themselves are married to some irascible and lustful man, they do not lose their dignity. They keep their composure even when they reveal their love to the stranger who visits them during the night, or when they submit to the fury of the father who finds them at fault. When their sorrow is too great, they bow their heads with such grace that, seeing them, one gets tears in one's eyes, and if they cry one becomes upset. But—are they enraged? Their attitude can repel. There they stand in a ladylike manner, the hand raised to ward off trouble, the face full of contempt. Do they give up? They bow submissively to their lover, their hands in the gesture of prayer. The Chinese shadow show succeeds like no other in transmitting to the viewer, through the movements of the figures, sensations and sentiments. Like no other, it can give us the illusion of an actual presentation of a human event.

In the Chinese shadow show it seems that there is no puppeteer; the figures on the screen live a life of their own. Max Buhrmann,[38] director of The Three Plum Blossoms Society in Germany, following the old Chinese tradition, affirms that often it

Young man from the Chinese province of Szechwan. The light passing through the figure lets one admire all the particular properties of a Chinese shadow figure: elegance and body grace, special attention to the costume's decorations, and subtly modulated colors. Above all, the limbs possess such capabilities as to give the figure unlimited mobility (PM).

its part taking some liberties. Improvisation, impromptu jokes and songs, allusions to problems of daily life were often addressed directly to the spectators.

The Chinese shadow show has no erotic elements. The reason for this can be found in the fact that, until the beginning of the twentieth century, it was the only theatrical entertainment for middle- and upper-class Chinese women. While Chinese men entertained themselves with people of doubtful principles, Chinese ladies invited shadow animators into their homes to amuse themselves, their children, and their servants.

Turkey

In Bursa, Anatolia, a headstone that still can be seen in the *hükùmet gáddesi* is inscribed: "To the magnet of the wise, to the patron who has many goals, to Mehmet Küscteri, master of the shadow show, nesting in paradise, inhabitant of celestial gardens." This sheik Küscteri was a dervish, a begging Islamic monk, who must have lived under the sultan Orchan (1326–1359). Sheik Küscteri is considered the inventor of the Turkish shadow show and the patron of shadow operators in Turkey. The story goes like this. Sultan Orchan had, among the workers at the construction site for the Bursa mosque, two cheerful masons named Hacivat and Karagöz. Their jokes kept the other laborers from working, and their indecent language irritated the sultan so much that he had them killed. What transpired then is what usually happens with the powerful: He missed the two clowns. As the story goes, had it not been for the dervish Mehmet Küscteri, who had immigrated from Persia, he would never have seen them again. Küscteri made a Hacivat and a Karagöz with camel's skins. He painted them, gave them movements, and put them behind a screen. In this way Sultan Orchan could again laugh at their jokes.

The Turkish shadow show always begins and ends with its two principal characters, Hacivat and Karagöz. After an introduction (*gösterme*) Hacivat appears on stage singing a song, and then he gives thanks to God and curses the Devil. Hacivat is an old and cultured *effendi* (gentleman) often characterized by his choppy manner of speaking, full of foreign words of Arabic and Persian origins. This is the way he talks to his friend Karagöz: "My Lord, your humble slave, who so highly values the importance of your indulgence, has come, confident in your high and respected dignity, singing some songs, to present homage to Your Excellent Lordship." Among the characters of the shadow show, Hacivat gets the most attention, thanks to his knowledge and education. What's more, he is considered the first *muktar* (leader) of his *mahalla* (city district). Being so knowledgeable and worldly, he can meet anyone who comes along with flattering courtesy. He is the complete opposite of Karagöz (also called Karakoz, Karagus, Karakus, Garagus, Karghus in Arab countries), who is almost exactly like the German Kasper. He has been assigned the part of an uneducated gypsy, who has rough and vulgar speech and regularly misunderstands Hacivat's words. No serious remarks can be made without Karagöz's comical comments. "Lacking self-control, Karagöz follows his natural instincts. Desiring women, he runs after them. He thoughtlessly engages himself in any extravagant adventure and disregards any given advice. He is afraid when facing danger but a braggart when it has disappeared." [40] Karagöz is the favorite of both the public and Hacivat, who, even though badly treated, cannot do without his gay companion. At one time Hacivat's wisdom triumphs over the carelessness of Karagöz. At another time, it is the roughness and the shrewdness of Karagöz that triumph over Hacivat's arid erudition. Karagöz has given his name to the Turkish shadow show and to its operator: *karagötsci*.

The largest part of the production occurs in front of Karagöz's house. Hacivat, with soft words, begs his dear friend to do him a favor and come out. Karagöz does so, annoyed, and a fight ensues. Then

94

Hacivat leaves and Karagöz complains and curses. Then Hacivat returns to Karagöz and the two make up. While Hacivat expresses his apologies he offers Karagöz every possibility to alter his words and interpret them in a bad sense. From the exchange of phrases and misunderstandings, it can be clearly seen that niether one has any money. To earn some, they decide to exercise a profession. They open up shop on the street as copyists; or Karagöz becomes a schoolteacher and Hacivat provides pupils. Or Karagöz proposes to enclose the heat of the summer and the cold of the winter in pipes and then to sell the heat in the winter and the cold in the summer. Or they become boatmen. Or they try to cure the possessed with exorcisms. With their problems, their shrewdness, and their confusion, they seem to be the predecessors of the movie comedians Laurel and Hardy.

The eleven parts of a Szechwan figure. Other figures may have fourteen or more elements. For example, they may have separate fingers or just a separate thumb.

Karagöz (literally, "black eye") is the principal character of the Turkish shadow theater. He is considered a gypsy and at times he greets the spectators with the gypsy greeting: Zombornos keros.

In the course of the show, various characters intervene. They are mocked by Karagöz and included in desperate adventures. Hacivat silences them with an abundance of words. They feel tricked by the two companions, and they wait for a chance to even the score. Almost always the same typical characters appear on the scene. This has a particular attraction for the spectator. He greets the figures as his old and dear acquaintances. The theater of Karagöz had, in its best periods, from fifty to sixty figures, and the shadow puppeteer chose a certain number of these for each comedy. "Every single figure is introduced with songs. These songs always mean an interruption of the dramatic presentation, and serve as a pause between the various scenes, so that each time a character or group of characters enters the stage, a new scene begins." [41]

The figures to be remembered are:

Bekri Mustafà: a rich peasant who comes to the city, goes around to the houses of ill-fame, and returns to his house drunk and dispossessed of everything, to meditate foolishly upon the world's wickedness.

Kawasse: another popular figure, who, with his large Turkish cap and his immaculate uniform, walks haughtily with his knees wide apart as if riding a horse. Even Karagöz always tries to disengage himself from this character.

Jahudi: a rich Jewish merchant with characteristically noble ways, whereas *Cifut* is a Jewish beggar who worked his way up from the lowest ranks. He is the one who procures the money and serves as pimp for Karagöz, who has only the lowest regard for him.

The Dervish: a smart rascal, who, behind the facade of piety and meditation, engages in the worst possible behavior.

Deli Bekir: one of the most important figures (known as Arnaut or the Albanian), a romantic character of a brigand (sometimes also representing the authorities), whose origin derives from the feared janizaries (slave soldiers) or from the elite body of the old Turkish army. Deli Bekir usually appears in

All Turkish shadow shows begin and end with Karagöz (shown in the illustration) and Hacivat. The animator can make puns or other veiled allusions, to the day's happenings or to politics. The theater of Karagöz was often the only critical voice in the Turkish Empire. It was continuously persecuted and its existence was directly related to the likes and dislikes of the sultan.

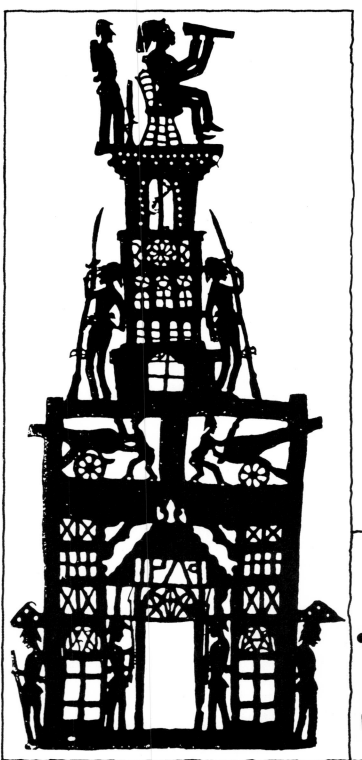

Old Egyptian figures for the shadow shows, found by Professor Paul Kahle in 1909 at Manzala in the Nile delta. They are of the highest artistic quality in the way they are perforated and colored; they resemble some Gothic windows.

The existence of shadow shows in Egypt dates back to the twelfth and thirteenth centuries when they must have been very popular. The only examples left from the dramatic poetry of the Arab Middle Ages are three shadow-show texts written by the Egyptian Ibn Danijal in 1270. Around the middle of the fifteenth century the sultan Tasciakmak, who was very religious, gave orders to burn all the shadow figures. But by the sixteenth and seventeenth centuries, Egyptian shadow animators were going to Turkey to present their shows. However, they were forced back by the Turkish theater of Karagöz. The animators were forced to retreat to small localities in the Nile delta. To safeguard their heritage, they learned the texts by heart and passed them on orally. The Egyptian shadow figures of the nineteenth and twentieth centuries developed different stylistic characteristics. The entire figure was colored and transparent, and, probably due to the Turkish influence, had some moving parts.

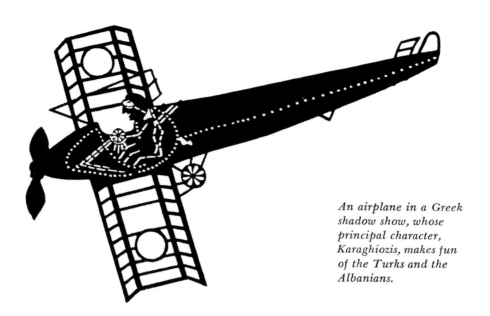

An airplane in a Greek shadow show, whose principal character, Karaghiozis, makes fun of the Turks and the Albanians.

Characters of the Turkish theater of Karagöz.

the finale when Karagöz has committed some terrible action. He grabs the sinner, who denies his bad behavior, and threatens him with the most horrible kind of death. At the end he is moved by the intercession of Hacivat and lets Karagöz go, in exchange for the promise to come back the following night to amuse the public.

Other important figures are *Beberuhi*, a midget, and *Çelebi*, often called only *Bei*, a well-dressed dandy.

The women characters appearing are: the none-too-faithful wives of Karagöz; the equally unfaithful wives of Hacivat; Hacivat's daughter, known as the fiancée, a young lady who willingly flirts with well-to-do men much older than herself; the ballerina; and others.

Also, there is the Arab; the Persian, who always appears on a horse; the Greek; the Armenian; and the Frenchman. All of them, each in his own way, mispronounce the Turkish language in a manner that makes the audience laugh.

The theater of Karagöz existed, at one time, in all parts of the Turkish Empire. In Greece we find it even today, in a more refined version, under the name *karaghiozis*. The presentations of the Karagöz show in Turkey and other Islamic countries are given during the early afternoon, usually during the month of Ramadan. The animator must be able to present at least thirty different comedies, one for each night of the month. In the shows, he always follows the traditions faithfully. The structure of the comedy is more important than its text, on which any puppeteer can improvise.

An animator of the theater of Karagöz at work. All the figures have a small hole in the shoulder area, through which passes a wooden rod twelve to sixteen inches long. In this way the figures are held on the screen. The animator, moving the rods around, obtains various movements: walking, bowing, leaning backward, and so on. Normally all the figures have only one hole, with the exception of Karagöz, who, as demonstrated in the bottom photo, has two.

100

Beberuhi, the midget of the Turkish shadow theater. A lamp is attached to his cap, and with it he searches for knowledge. Some midgets did service in the Turkish court as clowns, and besides other duties, they had to help their lord mount his horse by offering their hunched back as a stepping stool. In the figure's right shoulder there is a hole where a guiding rod is inserted. According to Islamic law, the representation of living creatures was not permitted; however, a figure with a hole through the body was not considered living (VB).

In color, the hero of the Javanese wajang kulit *shadow
theater. Centuries-old traditions have established
the characteristics of the figures. A strong and pimply
nose, round eyes, and a large mouth signify the
immeasurable strength of the hero. On the other hand,
a fine nose, flat forehead, small slanted eyes, and a closed
mouth indicate wisdom and distinction (figure in black
and white) (PM).*

Raden Harja Burisrawa   Resi Bisma   Batara Asmara

Figures of Wajang Purwa *of Central Java.*

during intermissions. The leaf is a representation of the past and future world, and at the same time the symbol of its creation. Like all of the one hundred and fifty to two hundred figures used for the presentation of *wajang kulit*, it is made from buffalo leather (*kulit* = "leather").

The sub-groups of *wajang kulit* are:

Wajang madja: Its events date back to the Madjapahit Javanese reign (fourteenth and fifteenth centuries).

Wajang gedog: Its content is taken from the Pangi legends (late Hindu era of Java), whose hero is Kuda-Wangheng-Pati.

Wajang purwa: Still very popular with all Indonesians. "At the center of *wajang purwa* presentations, there is Dasamuke, the Devil, who is feared by the gods and men for his violent acts. At last the god Vishnu intervenes and defeats him. The Devil promises to improve and to obey, and thus his life is spared. But very soon Dasamuka resumes his bad actions. There are numerous fights between Dasamuka (called Ravana) and Vishnu (in the guise of Rama). Ravana abducts Sita, Rama's wife, and hides her in his own palace in Ceylon. Rama's best allies are the prince of the monkeys, Hanuman, and the primate army, who fight desperately with the Devil and free Sita. Ravana is destroyed." [42]

The presentations of *wajang kulit* last from dusk

Batara Brama

Raden Anantaregia

Prabu Ramawigiagia

A gunungan

to dawn. The fine cotton screen (called *kelir*) is hung loosely in either a covered or a closed place. The *dalang* stays in front of the screen, and to his left and to his right are the figures, inserted by their guiding rods in the soft wood of a banana-tree log. The source of light, a bronze oil lamp shaped like a bird, hangs above the *dalang*. During the presentation the *dalang* swings it, giving to the shadow show a much more ghostly character. The *gamelan*, an orchestra which in its original form consisted of twenty to twenty-five men, sits around the puppeteer. Behind him are seated special guests and the adult men, who, from this position, have an unobscured view of the richly colored figures as they

Pa' Dogol, the principal comical figure of wajang kulit *in Malaysia.*

move. The women, seated on the opposite side of the screen, see the shadow show. The presentations are given for weddings, births, circumcisions, deaths, and even to exorcise evil spirits or to remove an illness.[43] The most recent form of *wajang kulit* is the Indonesian puppet theater. Also to be noted are *wajang golek,* with wooden rod marionettes; *wajang-klitik,* with flat figures, shaped and painted with sharp colors; and especially *wajang beber,* with illustrations and characters painted on paper.

MALAYSIA

In Malaysia, and particularly in the northern province of Kelantan, famous for its shadow show, it is the correspondence of movement to music that makes the show fascinating. Kelantan, even though it was under the rule of the king of Siam for a long time, was able to preserve its own traditions. In Kelantan two forms of *wajang kulit* exist. One, *wajang giava,* is somewhat similar in its technique,

Wajang golek *figure of Java.* Wajang, *meaning "shadow," is the main concept pertaining to all of the shows executed by figures behind a screen. About* wajang golek, *very little is known. We may speculate that its figures developed later than the primitive* wajang kulit, *from*

the Javanese shadow theater. In the west of Java, the preferred heroes and characters are those of the ancient Indian epics of the Ramayana *and* Mahabharata. *In the central part of the island, the subjects of the shows are based upon the deeds of the Arab prince Amir Hamzah, uncle of Muhammad (VB).*

figures, and repertoire to the Javanese *wajang purwa*. The other, *wajang siam,* as can be seen from its name, was influenced by the Siamese theater. This is evident in the appearance of about a hundred figures, most of them about thirty-two inches high. These are represented entirely in profile and have movable arms. The heroes are painted exactly as the Siamese tradition dictates: Rama's face, for example, green; that of Laksmana, yellow or brown.

The presentation is composed of one spoken part and one musical part.

> During the dialogue, the figures are presented rather statically: Only the arms are moved, while the figures' positions are changed very little. Only when the music begins do they start to move. The art of the *dalang* is to present a three-dimensional life combining simultaneously the two dimensions of the screen and its depth. By placing the figures at varying distances from the screen, the *dalang* obtains enlarged or decreased shadow images. . . . He holds a figure in each hand, making it move in full agreement with the course of events. At the same time, the trembling light lends perfect harmony to the figure together with unreal colors and rhythms, and slowly puts a spell on the spectator until he is completely unaware of what is happening. The *dalang* sings, talks, yells, acts crazy, and gets increasingly excited, until he reaches a trance-like state. His voice gradually rises and he is drawn into the magnetic sphere of his figures. Soon the identification is perfect: It is no longer the *dalang* who speaks, but rather the voice of the hero who performs, and he becomes a "medium." When it is late the presentation ends simply and everything quiets down.[44]

CAMBODIA

Where are the best seats at a shadow show? In front of the screen, through which we see shadows in colors or in black and white as in the shows of

Rama in his floating house.

China, Turkey, and Europe? Or behind the screen, on the operator's and orchestra's side, where the many colored figures face us (as they face the men of Java)? The Cambodian shadow theater is presented in front of the screen, together with the puppeteers, the orchestra, and the spectators. In back of the 24-foot-wide screen a burning fire provides light, and dancers move around with their leather boards. This show is called *robam nang sbel thom,* "dance of the large leather figures," abbreviated as *nang sbek,* because of the intricately incised buffalo-leather boards that the dancers hold high and move in accordance with the action.

In the *nang sbek* there are several movements that can be expressed with the dance: walking, marching, or flying, a struggle, meditation, mourning or sorrow, a meeting or war council, and, lastly, a metamorphosis. There are five categories of figures: princes (always in profile), princesses (always full

To the left: Above, scene from the Ramayana. *Below, the* dalang *during the scene produced above. The guiding rods of the figures in action are inserted in the soft wood of a banana-tree trunk. Thus the* dalang's *hands are free to move the figures' arms. The presentation is accompanied intermittently by the puppeteer's voice and by an orchestra whose music acts as a parallel rhythm.*

111

Cambodian nang sbek *figures on a large piece of leather:*
the fight between Laksmana and Indrajit. Their
movements correspond to ancient dances, for example,
those that are portrayed in temple decorations. Stylized
flames bring the scene to life.

Nang sbek *shadow show danced in Cambodia. Above: the army of monkeys is marching off for battle. Center: war council in Rama's palace; during this, the figures are not moved. Bottom: movement for "leaving for the battle." Right: Flying movement.*

113

face), monkeys, demons, and peasants. The figures make the prescribed movements to the accompaniment of thirteen musical pieces.[45]

Since the show lasts for seven nights, each night 150 boards with figures on them are shown several times; this gives the spectators a more lively and varied presentation. The show has at its disposal up to 150 boards with figures up to 6 feet high. These are all incised on one single bison skin with

Nang luong *figure of Thailand in the nineteenth century, representing Ravana's brother Kumphakan, the prince of the demons, standing on a snake. The figure is made from buffalo skin painted black, with some red, green, and transparent parts.*

Head of a hun *rod puppet of Thailand representing Rama's wife, Sita. It is presumed to be from the eighteenth century. The stupendous pagoda-shaped crown is inlaid with small rounded mirrors which, during the presentation, reflect the light and add to the splendor of the figure (PM).*

no movable parts, and it is up to the operator to show an entire scene on a space significantly narrowed by the several already mentioned figures.

Cambodia fell under Indian influence in the first century of the Volgar era. The Khmer culture is a mixture of Indian culture and primitive Cambodian culture. During the golden age of the Khmer reign, the Cambodian culture, so extraordinarily lively, became diffused into Siam (Thailand) and Laos. In its repertoire, the *nang sbek* presents *Rem Ker,* the Cambodian version of the Indian *Ramayana* epic, which shows the struggle of the good heroic king Preah Ream (Rama) to free his wife Seda (Sita), who has been abducted by the king of the demons, Prea Reap (Ravana); this battle always precedes any other presentation in the *nang sbek.* Preah Ream is backed up by his virtuous brother Preah Lak (Laksmana) and the monkey army that, thanks to the shrewdness of its leader, the white monkey Hanuman, is always victorious. The narrators (usually two) direct the presentation according to chosen episodes, as well as the dancers and the orchestra, composed of eight musicians. While the narrators explain the role of each figure and the action that is going to take place, the boards are not moved. Only when the music begins do the dancers enter into action and present by gestures what has already been narrated.

Besides the *nang sbek,* the Cambodians have another shadow theater, the *ayang* or *nang sbek tusc* (that is, "the small leathers") with movable figures. In the actions of these leather figures, the relationship to the *nang sbek* is evident, but in the figures themselves there are elements of style already familiar to us from the Malaysian Kelantan shadow show. The rods—the main rod fixed to the body and two rods fixed to the arms—are similar to those of the Chinese shadow show.

THAILAND

Only recently have the Cambodian shadow theater and that of Thailand been differentiated. Like Cambodia, Thailand also has two principal styles of shadow show. The *nang luong,* from the north, has great figures made from buffalo skin painted black. This show, like the related Cambodian *nang sbek,* presents Sanskrit epic poems from the *Mahabharata* and *Ramayana* called *Ramakien* ("praise to Rama"). However, the figures are moved mostly behind the screen, which can sometimes measure 60×12 feet. Another and rather recent style of Thailand shadow show is the *nang talung,* which originated in the southern province of Patalung. It is presented with 20-inch-high figures which are partly movable due to one, two, or three guide rods; the grotesque figures can move their lower jaws. In Thailand, in addition to the shadow shows, an extremely artistic rod puppet show, the *hun,* exhibits with success.

Creating Your Own
Puppet Shows

Actors and Puppeteers

The success of the puppet show depends on its basic premises (idea, text, direction), on scenic possibilities, and on the appearance of the puppets, but most of all on the puppeteer's ability to animate the figures. The quality of the presentation depends in great measure on the ability and artistry of the puppeteer. He has to have all the qualities of an actor, and, in addition, the attitudes necessary to make him an animator of motionless puppets. Like the actor in his role, he has to identify himself with the puppet and with its role. At times he is called upon to present not only one role but two or more at the same time, and for each one he has to express the respective character. To be able to concentrate exclusively on his role during the show, he has to be totally familiar with the technique of the puppet theater. This applies especially to the animator of marionettes or shadow figures, who often finds his marionette or his figure to be a complicated and capricious subject. For this it is very important that the animator continue to familiarize himself with his puppet and its characteristics, examining fully all its particularities and expressive possibilities. Even the simplest parts have to be rehearsed several times.

With his voice and appearance (which can be modified by masks and costumes) the actor acts directly on the spectator. The puppeteer also employs his own person and voice; however, he never presents himself in his real appearance, but rather with the puppet's. In this way the puppeteer has an advantage over the actor, since, through the puppet,

he can interpret any role: king, crocodile, devil, keeper of the temple, hero, mouse, clown, executioner, girl in love, death, ghost, star, talking tree, insect, or even a rabbit.

The Puppets

The presentation of these inanimate beings includes their manner of presentation and behavior. This does not originate from a simple imitation or reproduction, but from a creative simplification which exhibits few, but typical, gestures. The difference between reality and the puppet's representation of it is so great as to create new proportions. The head, which in man corresponds to approximately one seventh or one eighth the length of the body, in a puppet can reach up to one third of the puppet's height, and in the marionette up to a fifth or a sixth of it. Even the hands must be disproportionate, as are the eyes, which are made even bigger in proportion to the head.

The puppet finds life in movement and contrast. Contrasts are achieved with colors and the use of different materials that are brightened by the stage lighting. To represent hair and a beard, puppet makers do not use real hair or imitation hair, which would appear lifeless on the stage. Rather, they use wool threads, cord, tow, fur, coconut fiber. It would be a mistake to make the puppet's eyes resemble those of men or animals. A good substitute for the eye could well be a shiny round button which reflects the light. Contrasts are also made with real objects: a normal-sized bottle, a spoon, a pair of eyeglasses. These objects, in comparison with the puppet, ac-

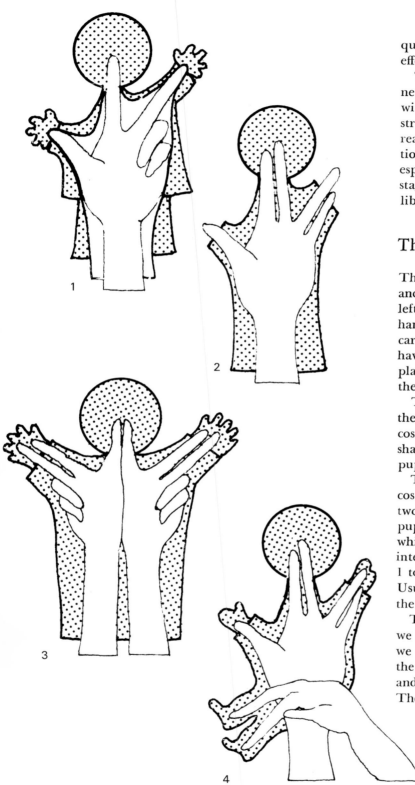

quire new proportions, producing a much stronger effect than they would have in their natural setting.

The following information on puppets, marionettes, and shadow shows is only suggestions. If used with a certain skill they can be enough for the construction of a small home theater. Those who have a real interest in this subject, and would like additional information, should refer to works devoted especially to the construction of puppets and to staging technique, which can be found in specialized libraries.

The True Puppet Show

The true puppet is composed of the head, the hands, and a shirt-like costume. Legs and feet are generally left out; when puppets do have legs they usually hang out from the stage. The head is usually of carved wood or a finished wooden geometrical form having a nose, mouth, and eyes. Papier-mâché and plastic materials are also widely used, especially for the head. Cloth is also used.

The neck and the head are perforated to permit the puppeteer to insert his finger. The shirt-like costume attached to the neck has a rectangular shape and must be roomy enough to allow the puppeteer's hand to move freely.

The sleeves are sewn to the extreme top of the costume. To the hands of the puppets are attached two little tubes used to make the arms longer. Many puppeteers, however, do without these tubes, which, while improving the shape of the puppet, often interfere with its movement. The drawings in Figs. 1 to 5 show how the puppet is placed on the hand. Usually the index finger is inserted into the head, the thumb and the middle finger into the arms (Fig. 1).

There are also other possibilities. For example, if we insert the index and middle finger into the head we can move it around without moving the rest of the puppet. In this case the thumb, the ring finger, and the little finger are inserted into the arms (Fig. 2). The body symmetry of the puppet is not disturbed by

5a

5b

5c

5d

5e

5f

any bent fingers. In bigger puppets it is possible to use both hands (Fig. 3). With these it is possible to grab objects of a certain size. If the thumb is moved, the puppet moves its head.

The legs—which often interfere with the show—are easily made of stuffed cloth. They can be moved with the fingers of either hand (Fig. 4).

When there are animal figures in the show (Figs. 5a to 5f), the hands are adapted to the forms of the animals.

The true puppets are shown to the spectator above a curtain which hides the puppeteer. Such a curtain can be simply a stretched canvas across a door. Or one can build a small table stage with

stage, curtain, and sides on hinges to save space (Fig. 6, page 120, shows the inside). It can be made of plywood srtengthened by wood strips. To the strip on top is attached the curtain rod. The bottom strip can also be used as a guide for the figures of the shadow show (see page 130). It can be used to attach lateral or movable scenes in puppet and marionette shows; the same theater can be used for the shadow show by adding only a floor. At the same height as the bottom strip, on the folding sides, there are two other strips attached, one on the left and one on the right, where the floor is placed when the theater is used for the marionette show. A strip less than a yard long is sufficient to

119

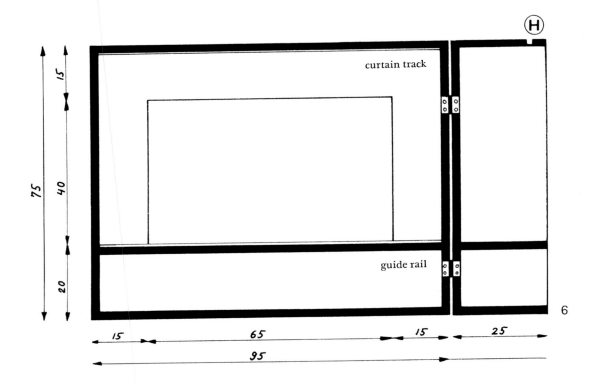

attach the back part of the stage; if the theater is used for a shadow show, a lamp is attached. For the back part of the stage it is necessary to choose a light, transparent material: Through it we are able to see the public and the puppets without being seen ourselves. The strip is inserted on the left and the right sides of the portion shown in Diagram H. This gives the theater a solid structure.

The lighting for a puppet or marionette show can be obtained from a strong office light reflecting on the front of the scene. For a presentation to be given in front of an audience of a certain size it is necessary to have a theater or a curtain where one or more puppeteers can stand up. In a presentation it is important to see how the spectators are seated. It is advantageous to have the spectators look slightly upward or horizontally. For this reason chil-

dren should not be seated too close; otherwise they will see only the top of the puppet; in small rooms it is advisable to use a table theater.

The puppeteer lifts the puppet above the curtain so that it is visible from the knees up. It is important for the puppeteer to keep his forearm steady and perfectly perpendicular and not to let the puppet drop too low; the head of the puppet cannot bend backward; the index finger that holds it has to be slightly bent toward the audience. To have the puppet bend his body, the puppeteer has to bend his hand; to make it nod its head, he has only to move the finger that directs the head; other simple movements are grabbing, holding objects, and bowing. Even though these movements and gestures seem very simple, it is necessary for the puppeteer to keep practicing.

120

Two puppets of the Théâtre des Amis established by the French writer George Sand with her son in the castle at Nohant (Indre) in 1847. That theater with its artistically carved puppets offered to a chosen circle of artists and writers of the time the possibility of witty, satirical parody of daily happenings and human vanity (ML).

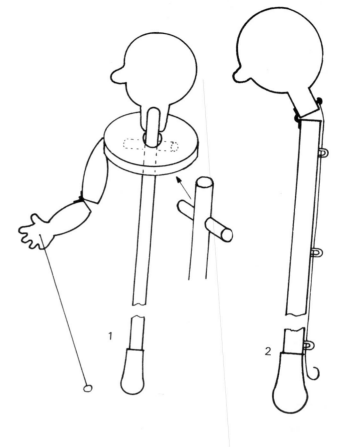

The Rod Puppet Show

Rod puppets can be simply made out of corks and
ladles. Imaginative mothers can paint on a face and
dress them up in their own costume. The difference
between these children's puppets and the puppets
of *wajang golek* or *wajang klitik* is, naturally, great.

A simple type of rod puppet was used by the
Hänne Theater, established in Cologne in 1806.
This puppet is twenty-four inches high and is attached to a solid rod. One arm is moved from beneath by a string; the other arm hangs motionless.
The skeleton of this puppet shows two wood strips
crossing the main rod. One represents the shoulders,
where the arms are attached; the other the hips,
where the legs are attached. With this kind of pup-

122

pet it is possible to create a very suggestive presentation. With minor technical tricks it is possible to
improve the structure of these puppets. The arms
can be attached to an oval-shaped collar piece,
which leaves the main rod loose, so that the head
can be moved without moving the rest of the puppet (Fig. 1). The head can also be bent forward
(Fig. 2). We can even attach guide strings to the arms
of these manikins, as has been done in the rod puppets of Russia and Czechoslovakia. One must remember, however, that maneuvering these puppets
becomes more difficult, since one hand holds the
puppet and the other has to guide the movement.
The rod puppet shows require two or three puppeteers, since one puppeteer can animate only one
puppet at a time.

Head of a Thai puppet from Bangkok, nineteenth or
twentieth century. The traditional hun *show disappeared*
as popular dramatic theater at the beginning of the
twentieth century, but it is possible that it is still cultivated
among learned people in Thailand. The works of the rod
puppet theater have been taken over by the traditional
danced dramas (VB).

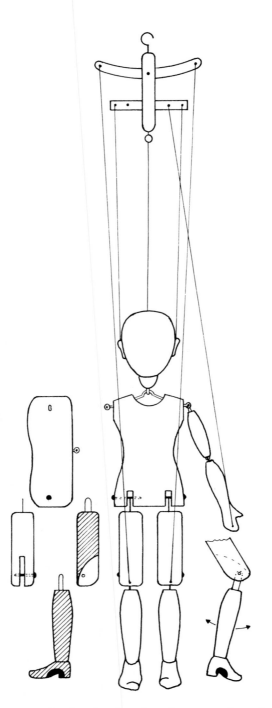

The marotte, *closely related to the rod puppet, shown in its simplest form. The hand of the puppeteer is an essential element of the* marotte, *especially when the puppet is dressed and the puppeteer hides beneath its costume. In this case, his hand is visible.*

The Marionette Show

The marionette has to be movable. Its movements reproduce, in a simple form, those of a living being. It is for this reason that the marionette is built much like the skeleton of the living creature being represented. Like a skeleton, the puppet is an assembly of single parts joined together. The marionette is composed of a head, body, and limbs. Those puppets resembling a human being have a body with movable hips, head, arms, and legs. It is for the maker to decide if elbows, knees, hands, and feet are also to be articulated. The marionette's limbs are moved by strings. These are connected to the so-called guiding cross. Its movement possibilities are many, and the puppeteer must determine which form of guiding cross is most comfortable for his method of presentation and for the marionette's mobility. A marionette representing an animal—for example, a bird—has a guiding cross different than that used for a circus clown. For very simple marionettes only seven strings are used, as shown by the illustration. With these strings the marionette can move its head, body, arms, and legs (in other words, it can walk). More strings are added if a more complicated movement is desired. Usually, the puppeteer holds in one hand the guiding cross and with the other hand pulls the strings. Many movements can be obtained by the simple manipulations of the guiding cross. The marionette in the illustration will bow when the guiding cross is inclined forward.

The movements of the puppet are controlled by gravity; for this reason the relation between the total weight of the marionette and its components is very important. The illustrated marionette is sculpted in wood and the weight of its components can be easily controlled. The total weight of a marionette should never exceed 4.4 pounds, since handling a heavier puppet will tire a marionettist. Conversely, a very light marionette could not be animated properly and could also be easily moved by the slightest air current. A marionette for a table

Burmese marionette of 1900. The head and hands are of papier-mâché; the hair is real human hair. Animals and human beings have an almost equal importance in the Burmese marionette theater. While the animals are represented as caricatures, the human form is represented accurately and its costumes richly decorated. The faces, however, do not have special characteristics and give the impression of being masks. The only exceptions are the comical characters (VB).

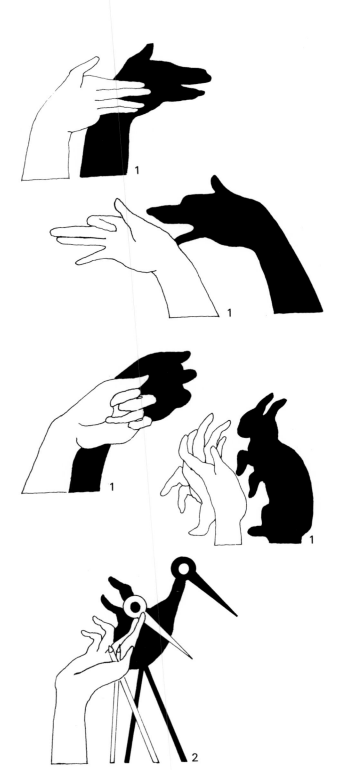

stage can be only eight to ten inches tall; one that has to be used in larger theaters, twelve inches; for theater use in schools and similar places, sixteen inches. It is surprising how even small marionettes can be easily seen from a distance as long as they are sufficiently illuminated.

Shadow Shows

The simplest shadow show is obtained by the projection of the hand's shadow against a white wall (Fig. 1). These shadows can be easily improved by holding small objects (Fig. 2).

Various figures can also be cut out of paper or cardboard so as to have a complete and ready collection (Fig. 3).

Another rather simple shadow show can be made as follows: About two inches behind a screen stretched in front of a door, place a light, keeping the room where the spectators are seated in the dark. The rest is left to the imagination of the animator. Different objects and cut figures can be easily used, since even the simplest forms and objects have a remarkable effect when seen as shadows.

The true shadow show's setting much resembles the latter example. The figures are placed behind an illuminated screen, in front of which the audience is seated. The screen is a cloth or drawing paper stretched on a frame. The puppeteer holds his figures between the light and the screen; at times he moves his figures right up against the screen. The source of light is placed beside him or above his head so as not to interfere with his work. One must remember that the shadows will be more strongly marked depending upon the distances between the light, figures, and screen. The closer the figures and the light are to the screen, the clearer are the shadows. The further they are from the screen, the less clear are the shadows; however, they will acquire gigantic proportions.

There are two kinds of figures for the shadow show: the colored and the black. For the former,

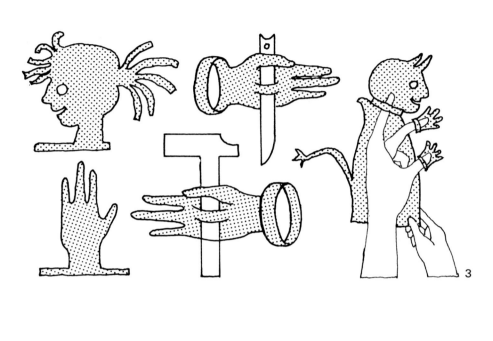

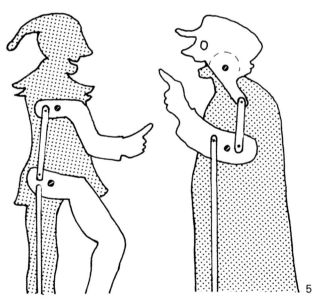

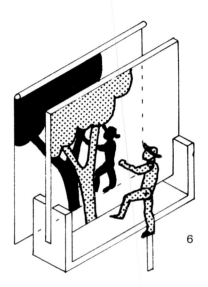

6

7

transparent material (sheets of plastic are good) painted with translucent colors is used. The black figures are obtained from any of a great variety of opaque materials: e.g., cardboard, thin wood, leather. These figures can be given eyes, hair, and other features by perforating holes in them. Strings are also attached to the figures to animate them from beneath (Fig. 4). A more experienced person can also create different movements (Fig. 5).

The scenery is made by cutting out cardboard or by pasting together several sheets of transparent paper. The latter method would give shadows of different density. These scenic decorations can be inserted between two glass plates and mounted on a permanent frame (Fig. 6). Or the scenery can be drawn on old film or on plates of glass that can be inserted into a slide projector (Fig. 7).

The same stage can be used as that described for the true puppets. A frame, on which can be stretched a transparent cloth approximately sixteen

by twenty-six inches, is also necessary. In the pre-ceeding chapter we have already described how the figures of the shows of Asia are guided from beneath. Although this technique is feasible, a much simpler way is recommended to enable the animator to handle more than one figure at the same time. An important element of this method is the guide rail. It consists of two strips of wood, about one inch wide and 2/10 inches thick, nailed about 1/10 inch apart to form a track along the length of the stage or screen (Fig. 8, page 130). The figures that have been provided with extensions, as shown in the same draw-ing, are inserted into this track and easily guided by only one hand. Adding a third strip, one can obtain a second track, which facilitates handling several figures at the same time. To keep the fig-ures on the track, it is sufficient to attach a small piece of wood or cardboard to the back of the ex-tension, as shown in Fig. 9. The guide rail can also be used for movable scenes.

*Marionettes created in 1918 by Sophie Taeuber-Arp for the
presentation by the Zurich School of Arts and Trades of
"Re Cervo" by Carlo Gozzi. The figures were made by
Carl Fischer. He gave them a big round body with a thin
neck and a small head. The king and the guards were
given a metallic shine; the lady a porcelain white; the
courtiers were painted gray and violet; the intriguers were
given a strident red or a yellow-blue contrast reflecting
their changeable and fickle hearts (KG).*

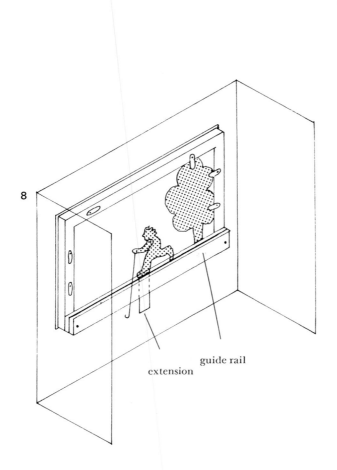

8

guide rail

extension

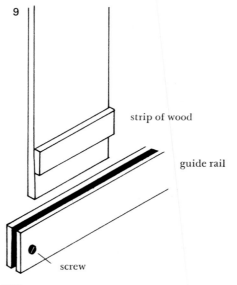

9

strip of wood

guide rail

screw

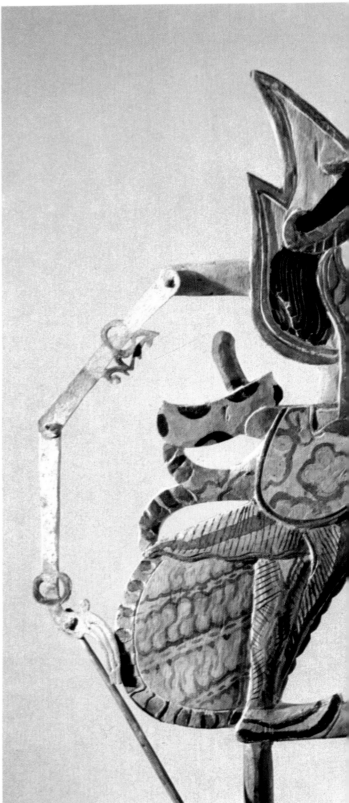

Wajang klitik *figure from Java. The word which signifies shadow is not applicable in this case, since this presentation is not done with shadows, but with wooden puppets. The word* klitik *signifies small, thin, skinny. Actually, the figures are not as big as those of the shadow shows, and unlike those of* wajang golek, *which are made to resemble the body form, these figures are made of very thin wood, about one fifth of an inch thick. The figures are then painted and decorated in gold (PM).*

NOTES

1. René Simmen. *Der Mechanische Mensch.* Zurich, 1967.
2. *Ibid.*
3. Richard Pischel. *Die Heimat des Puppenspiels.* Halle, 1900.
4. Paul McPharlin, in *The Puppet-Theatre in America* (New York, 1949), indicates the first presentations in America date back to 1524, the work of a clown puppeteer who arrived with Hernando Cortez.
5. Sergei Obraszov. *The Puppeteer's Trade.* Moscow, 1950.
6. Adolf Robert Stemmle. *Die Zuflöte.* Berlin, 1940.
7. H. Netzle. *Das Süddeutsche Marionetten-Wandertheater.* Munich, 1938.
8. Sergius Golowin. *Das Tarot.* Zurich, 1968.
9. J. B. Frisch. *Deutsch-lateinisches Wörterbuch.* Berlin, 1741.
10. A study by the *Das Puppentheater* magazine. Leipzig, 1931.
11. George Speaight. *Punch & Judy.* London, 1970. See also George Speaight. *History of the English Puppet-Theatre.* London, 1955.
12. Peter Fraser. *Punch and Judy.* London, 1970.
13. Prince Hermann Pückler-Muskau. *Briefe eines Verstorbenen.* Stuttgart, 1836.
14. Felix Benoit. *Lyon Secret.* Lyons, 1971.
15. Henri Leroudier. *Lyon Guignol.* Lyons, 1970.
16. Paul Louis Mignon. *Marionettes–Marionette Theater.* Lausanne, 1963.
17. André-Charles Gervais. *Marionnettes et Marionnettistes de France.* Paris, 1947.
18. Mignon, *op. cit.*
19. Charles Magnin. *Histoire des Marionnettes.* Paris, 1852.
20. Frisch, *op. cit.*
21. Philipp Leibrecht. *Zeugnisse und Nachweise zur Geschichte des Puppenspiels in Deutschland.* Dissertation, Freiburg in Br., 1918.
22. H. S. Rehm. *Buch der Marionetten.* Berlin, 1905.
23. Leibrecht, *op. cit.*
24. Edmund Stadler, in Merker-Stammler, *Reallexikon der Deutschen Literatur-Geschichte,* Vol. 111.
25. Carl Engel. *Deutsche Puppenkomödien,* Vol. IV, Oldenburg, 1876.
26. Günter Böhmer. *Puppentheater.* Munich, 1969.
27. E. T. A. Hoffman. *Seltsame Leiden eines Theaterdirektors.* 1818.
28. Mignon, *op. cit.*
29. Alfred Altherr. *Marionetten.* Erlenbach-Zurich, 1926. See also Alfred Altherr. *Schatten- und Marionettenspiele.* Zurich, 1923.
30. Information by Peter Gysin, Editor of *Puppenspiel und Puppenspieler.* Riehen (Basel), 1971.
31. Maria Piper, "Bunraku," in *Atlantis.* Zurich, A. XI.
32. Adolf Muschg, "Bunraku," series on the Japanese theater in *Neue Zürcher Zeitung.* Zurich, 1967.
33. Littman. *Arab Shadow Shows.*
34. Wang Hsun. Dept. of Applied Art. Peking, 1956.
35. Georg Jakob. *Geschichte des Schattentheaters.* Hanover, 1925.
36. Berthold Laufer. *Chinesische Schattenspiele.* Munich, 1915.
37. Karl H. Henking, "Shadow Theater in Asia," in *Puppenspiel und Puppenspieler,* No. 36. Basel, 1970.
38. Max Bührmann. *Das Farbige Schattenspiel.* Berne, 1955.
39. Laufer, *op. cit.*
40. Georg Jakob. *Das Türkische Schattentheater.* 1900.
41. Helmut Ritter. *Karagös, Türkische Schattenspiele.* Hanover, 1924. See also Otto Spies. Introduction to *Türkisches Puppentheater.* Emsdetten, 1959.
42. Gerd Höpfner. *Südostasiatische Schattenspiele,* museum guide. Berlin, 1967.
43. Carl Hagemann. *Spiele der Völker.* Berlin, 1919.
44. *Jacques Brunet. Wayang-Kulit (Kelantan).* International Institute for the Study and Documentation of Comparative Music. Berlin, 1971.
45. Jacques Brunet. *Nang Sbek.* Berlin, 1969.

SELECTED BIBLIOGRAPHY

Baird, Bill. *The Art of the Puppet.* New York, 1966.

Blackham, Olive. *Shadow Puppets.* London, 1960.

Chesnais, Jacques. *Histoire Générale des Marionnettes.* Paris, 1947.

D'Allemagne, Henri René. *Histoire des Jouets.* Paris, 1902.

Jakob, Georg. *Geschichte des Schattentheaters.* Hanover, 1925.

Leydi, Roberto and Renata M. *Marionette e Burattini.* Milan, 1958.

Maindron, Ernest. *Marionnettes et Guignols.* Paris, 1908.

Mignon, Paul Louis. *Marionnettes.* Lausanne, 1963.

H. Siegfried Rehm. *Das Buch der Marionetten.* Berlin, 1905.

Sézan, Claude. *Les Poupées Anciennes.* Neufchâtel, 1929.

UNIMA (Union Internationale des Marionnettes). *Puppet Theater in the World.* Prague, 1965.

135